D1266287

DANTE *and the* BLESSED VIRGIN

DANTE
and the
BLESSED VIRGIN

RALPH McINERNY

University of Notre Dame Press
Notre Dame, Indiana

Copyright © 2010 by University of Notre Dame
Notre Dame, Indiana 46556
www.undpress.nd.edu
All Rights Reserved

Manufactured in the United States of America

Library of Congress Cataloging-in-Publication Data

McInerny, Ralph M.
Dante and the Blessed Virgin / Ralph McInerny.
p.   cm.
Includes bibliographical references and index.
ISBN-13: 978-0-268-03517-4 (cloth : alk. paper)
ISBN-10: 0-268-03517-2 (cloth : alk. paper)
1. Dante Alighieri, 1265–1321—Criticism and interpretation.   2. Dante Alighieri,
1265–1321—Characters—Mary, Blessed Virgin, Saint.   3. Mary, Blessed Virgin,
Saint—In literature.   I. Title.
PQ4419.M2M35   2010
851'.1—dc22
                    2009041749

♻ *This book is printed on recycled paper.*

ACC LIBRARY SERVICES
AUSTIN, TX

For

Cathy, Mary, Anne, Nancy, Beth, Amy,
Terrill, Ellen, Clare, Lucy, Rita,
and Vivian

Sed certe ad hoc opus nimiam omnino fateor esse meam insufficientiam, propter nimiam materiam incomprehensibilitatem, propter nimiam scientiae meae tenuitatem, propter nimiam linguae meae indignitatem, et propter nimiam personae laudandae laudem et laudabilitatem.

Certainly I must confess my utter insufficiency to write this book—because of the matter, difficult of comprehension; because of the thinness of my knowledge; because of the unworthiness of my syle; and because of the profound praise due the person to be honored.

—*Speculum Beatae Mariae Virginis*, prologus

CONTENTS

PROLOGUE

One of the marvels of art is that our appreciation of it does not require that we share the outlook of the artist. There must, of course, be sympathy, and more than sympathy, with the protagonist and with his manner of viewing his plight. A reader in the third millennium can be drawn into a Greek tragedy and experience the anguish of a character whose culture is utterly alien to his own. Explanations of this have been advanced. It requires a willing suspension of disbelief, a dismissal of the differences, and then immersion in a plot involving decisions almost wholly foreign in their weight and gravitas to those that engage the latter-day reader. *Almost* wholly foreign. What counterpart in our times could there be, *pace* Freud, to the dilemma of Oedipus? Nonetheless, it may well be said that beneath the undeniable strangeness is the note of familiarity, a familiarity due to our common humanity. The great imaginative works bring about in us a sense of affinity with agents living in cultural circumstances long since gone.

But we need not appeal only to the chronologically distant. When we read Conrad's *Heart of Darkness*, the mesmerizing voice of the narrator establishes a rapport with such a one as Kurtz, a Kurtz who, alive or dead, we could never be. Moreover, we grasp the contrast between a Europe that no longer exists and a colonial Africa that is no more. It seems not to matter at all that those referents no longer exist.

Call our empathy aesthetic, in the best sense of the term. For the duration of the story, we sense and feel that the protagonist is ourselves and we are him. We reach across the differences and in some way we are one with Kurtz, *notre semblable, notre frère*.

I think, too, of Matthew Arnold's "Dover Beach." One who does not share the poet's interpretation of the way in which Christianity is the putative casualty of nineteenth-century philology and science can nonetheless occupy the outlook of the poem and be stirred.

> The Sea of Faith
> Was once, too, at the full, and round earth's shore
> Lay like the folds of a bright girdle furled.
> But now I only hear
> Its melancholy, long, withdrawing roar,
> Retreating, to the breath
> Of the night-wind, down the vast edges drear
> And naked shingles of the world.

One can argue with Arnold's prose work on these matters, but the argument of the poem requires only our responding to the feelings that would accompany holding Arnold's melancholy views, and we experience a similar *frisson*.

Great imaginative works enable us to sense a common humanity with those with whom we have almost nothing else in common. But it would not do to suggest that there is just some residue of common nature that remains when all the differences have been thought away. Appreciation of the story requires that, for a time, we take on an outlook and occupy circumstances that have little to do with our own lives.

All this is fanfare for the way we read Dante. I have sometimes been struck, at meetings of medievalists, by the way in which the beliefs of those long ago days are discussed with perceptiveness and intelligence, but also with the unstated sense that we are dealing with matters no longer believed, indeed, incredible. Aesthetically, from the vantage point of the scholar, surpassed attitudes can be reoccupied and things said of pith and moment. Once, however, I listened to a somewhat facetious talk having to do with medieval Eucharistic treatises, and it occurred to me to remark that there were those of us in the audience who shared the beliefs of the authors of those treatises. This was not criticism, nor was it an irrelevant remark. I have come to think that there can be an advantage—it is a possibility only, nothing inevitable—in sharing the deepest beliefs of an author whose assumptions must otherwise be taken on only in an aesthetic and scholarly way.

Dantisti, as a group, seem to me to be a very special breed of scholar. Those whom I have come most to admire, whatever their personal attitude toward the Catholic faith that animates all the work of the great Florentine, seem to possess an uncanny ability to enter into Dante's world in a way that strains against a merely aesthetic identification. Chaucer makes fewer demands in this regard, I think, and of course Shakespeare is notoriously ambiguous as to his own beliefs. But there is no such doubt possible in the case of Dante. He is inescapably and thoroughly Catholic. A Catholic who reads him, one who shares the same faith, can be in a privileged position.

It would be absurd, of course, to suggest that believing as Dante does enables one, just for that reason, to better appreciate him. It would be absurd to suggest that all the Dantisti who do not share the great Florentine's faith are thereby consigned to some outer darkness. And some scholars, such as Etienne Gilson and Ernest Fortin, have argued from a Catholic perspective for the heterodoxy of Dante's Catholicism. For all that, the theme of this little book, Dante and the Blessed Virgin, provides a Catholic reader with a unique opportunity to respond to this central element of the great poet's work in a way that goes far beyond scholarly or aesthetic appreciation. It is somewhat like the different ways in which a believing or nonbelieving reader responds to Gerard Manley Hopkins's poem "The Blessed Virgin Compared to the Air We Breathe," which ends:

> Be thou then, O thou dear
> Mother, my atmosphere;
> . . . .
> World-mothering air, air wild,
> Wound with thee, in thee isled,
> Fold home, fast fold thy child.

I have found a few works devoted explicitly to the role of the Blessed Virgin in Dante, not all of them by Catholics. There is a little book of Hellmut Schnackenburg, a marvelous study by Jaroslav Pelikan, and moving little books by Domenico Bassi and Renato Nicodemo.[1] They are, in their different ways, edifying. That is what Dante aimed at explicitly in the *Divine Comedy*: to move us from the misery of sin to the happiness of salvation. And he emphasized the essential providential role of Mary in helping us to make that transition.

The Catholic can see Dante's devotion to the Blessed Virgin in warm continuity with his or her own beliefs and practices. Central as Mary is to the *Divine Comedy*, she has become even more central in Catholic belief in the centuries since it was written. In the seventeenth century, St. Louis-Marie Grignion de Montfort wrote that the role of Mary in the life of the Church would become ever more pronounced in what he called "these last days."[2] And Father Frederick Faber ended his preface to the English translation of de Montfort's work with a prayer for the "speedy coming of that great age of the Church which is to be the Age of Mary!" The prophesy has been fulfilled and the prayer answered. Pope John Paul II's personal motto— "Totus tuus sum Maria" (Mary, I am all yours)—had a Montfortian ring to it.

The nineteenth century saw the Catholic definition of Mary's Immaculate Conception and the twentieth century the definition of the Assumption of Mary, body and soul, into heaven. We might link the first with Mary's appearance to Bernadette at Lourdes in the mid-nineteenth century, where she identified herself as "I am the Immaculate Conception." There is less of a link between the dogma of the Assumption and the visions of Mary by three shepherd children at Fatima, Portugal, in the early twentieth, but the official Church sanction of those apparitions is eloquent of Mary's unique role in our salvation. Perhaps the present century will see the definition of Mary as Mediatrix of all Graces. Such definitions are a corroboration of the faith of the Church. Dante and millions of others believed these truths about Mary without any official definition of them.

Some have responded to these definitions as if they were novelties introduced into Christian faith, but they are not. Ours is an apostolic faith, and our beliefs accordingly must be in warm and essential continuation with the deposit of faith entrusted to the Apostles. Any conception of the development of doctrine that ignored this connection would be wrong. One of the saddest things in human history has been the divisions among those who are Christians. No one, I think, addressed the misgivings of non-Catholics to the development of Marian doctrine more effectively than Charles De Koninck.[3] As a very young man, he wrote a little book addressing the way in which certain scriptural passages from the Canticle of Canticles and from the Wisdom books are applied to the Blessed Virgin Mary in the liturgy.[4] One could make a small florilegium of those attributions from the Little Office of the Blessed Virgin. And of course, there is the Litany of the Blessed Virgin. To find such devotion to Mary, such insistence on her unique role, excessive is to fail to see the nature of the history of salvation.

~ I would have been less than frank if I had not begun with these few animadversions, which explain, if they do not justify, why such an amateur as myself would dare to produce yet another book on Dante. Jorge Luis Borges, a lapsed Catholic but perhaps at the end reconciled, like Dante's figure of Buonconte in the *Purgatorio*, said this with reference to the essay "Introduction à un poème sur Dante" by Paul Claudel: "Claudel has written—in a page unworthy of Paul Claudel—that the spectacles awaiting us after death will no doubt little resemble those that Dante showed us in the *Inferno*, the *Purgatorio*, and the *Paradiso*."[5] That is a large subject, and there is much with which one might quibble in this essay by that greatest of modern Catholic poets,[6] but there is also much in it to ponder and to praise, not least Claudel's comparison of a *philosophia perennis* and a *poesis perennis*, the latter exemplified by Dante and the *Comedy*. Few things could be more profitable than comparing Santayana's *Three Philosophical Poets* and this essay of Paul Claudel. Poets like Claudel are in the direct line from Dante Alighieri.

Like his great predecessor, John Paul II, Pope Benedict XVI has taken to ending his encyclicals with an explicit reference to the Blessed Virgin. The final paragraph of *Spe Salvi* (*Saved in Hope*) is entitled "Mary, Star of Hope." Benedict begins with a discussion of the *Ave maris stella* and links Mary's role to the stars by which sailors would navigate the sea. Life is a journey, and "Who more than Mary could be a star of hope for us? With her 'yes' she opened the door of our world to God himself; she became the living Ark of the Covenant, in whom God took flesh, became one of us, and pitched his tent among us (cf. John 1:14)."

NOTE ON TRANSLATIONS, EDITIONS, AND ABBREVIATIONS

Prosaic language easily gives way to translation, to a restatement in equally impersonal words. Euclid alone may have looked on beauty bare, as Edna St. Vincent Millay said, but who has not learned his Euclid in translation? Logicians speak disdainfully of natural languages, supposedly rife with ambiguity, and urge upon us the merits of their austere *p*'s and *q*'s. But there are uses of language which resist being turned into another form, let alone another language. Preeminent among them is poetry. Whenever language is something other than a pure medium, what is being said becomes inseparable from the how.

For many years I taught a course called "Dante and Aquinas." St. Thomas attracts translators in the dozens; it is difficult to resist the temptation to carry over into English that limpid prose. Having succumbed to it myself, I have learned how difficult a task translation can be. It can be done, more or less well or badly, but the conviction grows on the reader of the *Divine Comedy* that, while this work may be disguised in other languages, it resists the effort. Nevertheless, translations of Dante multiply, although every translator seems somewhat sheepish about what he or she has done. The suggestion is that while the reader may make do with Dante in English, or French, or German, finally, Dante can speak to us only in the original.

In the course I mentioned I was always concerned that the students had before them the originals, Thomas in Latin and Dante in Italian. This was not meant to turn them into pedants but rather to provide the occasion for hearing the original voices of our two authors. In recent years, Patrick Gardner served as my course assistant and generously offered to give quick crash courses in Latin and Italian—in the evenings, with attendance quite voluntary. All but one or two students availed themselves of that opportunity. It takes a long time before one can easily read the *Comedy* in the original, much less all the explanatory notes. But one can, like T. S. Eliot, begin reading Dante even before knowing any Italian, enjoying its music before grasping its meaning.

In what follows, I almost always provide the original Italian of Dante before an English version of it. Unless otherwise noted, these English translations are my own. The originals on which I rely are

> Dante Alighieri. *Commedia*. Con il commento di Anna Maria Chiavacci Leonardi. 3 vols. Vol. 1, *Inferno*; Vol. 2, *Purgatorio*; Vol. 3, *Paradiso*. Milan: Arnaldo Mondadori, 1991. (This became my preferred edition; Chiavacci Leonardi's notes and comments are invariably helpful.)

> Dante Alighieri. *Vita Nova*. A cura Luca Carlo Rossi, Introduzione Guglielmo Gorni. Milan: Arnoldo Mondadori, 1999.

> Dante Alighieri. *Tutte le opere*. A cura di Luigi Blasucci. Florence: G. C. Sansoni Editore, 1981. For the *Convivio* and the *Letter to Can Grande*.

English translations of St. Thomas Aquinas and other Latin and Italian sources are also my own. Biblical quotations generally follow *The Holy Bible*, New American Catholic Edition (New York: Benziger Brothers, 1952). In referring to Psalms I provide the Vulgate number and the alternate numbering of the Hebrew text.

Abbreviations in the chapters include:

Ep. 13	*Epistole* 13 (Dante's *Letter to Can Grande*)
Inf.	*Inferno*
Par.	*Paradiso*
Purg.	*Purgatorio*
ST	Thomas Aquinas, *Summa theologiae*
VN	*Vita Nuova*

ONE

A New Life Begins

La donna gentile: The gentle lady

The Blessed Virgin Mary is the key to Dante. We find her there behind the scenes at the very beginning of the *Commedia*, since it is her compassion for the wandering poet that sets the great journey in motion, through intermediaries; we find her there at the end in the magnificent closing cantos of the *Paradiso*, the very gate of heaven. And, as we shall see, her role becomes ever more explicit throughout the great poem. In the *Vita Nuova*, an earlier work of Dante, Mary is present as the object of the young Beatrice's devotion, a devotion that is contagious, although it is difficult to think that Dante was ever entirely devoid of it. With his love for Beatrice, for her beauty, and for her virtue, that devotion intensifies, and after her death—not immediately, to be sure, but only after and despite dalliance with another woman, whom he treats as a mere bagatelle in the *Vita Nuova*[1] and puts to allegorical purpose in another earlier work, the *Convivio*—his love for Beatrice finally emerges in his great poem as the means of his salvation. Lost in a dark wood, threatened by the beasts within him, he acknowledges that after Beatrice's death he had fallen into vices

1

that endangered his soul. In the *Vita Nuova*, his love for Beatrice is filtered through the requirements of courtly love and only gradually transcends them. In the *Comedy*, Beatrice's role in Dante's conversion, in his salvation, is given immortal expression.

So isn't it Beatrice, not Mary, who is the key to Dante? There are moments in the *Vita Nuova* when the two seem almost to fuse, and the reader feels uneasiness at certain descriptions of Dante's beloved in which the devotee is almost identified with the object of her devotion. The two women are inseparably linked, and in the *Comedy* they will be joined with another, St. Lucy; Dante scholars will write of the *tre donne*, the three women, and for good reason, as we shall see. But the preeminence of Mary is never in doubt. To call Mary Dante's alpha and omega would be too much, of course: her role is always that of a mediatrix. It is in her Son, her spouse, her creator, that Dante's heart will find its rest. At the end of the *Comedy*, Dante, thanks to Mary's intercession, is given a glimpse of the Trinity, of the "love that moves the sun and other stars," and returns to recount his journey. The *Divine Comedy* is the poetic expression of the journey any sinner must make if he would realize his very reason for being.[2]

The sublimation of Dante's love for Beatrice in the *Vita Nuova* and the poet's transfiguration of his beloved might tempt us to think that the role of Mary, too, is largely a poetic device. There have been quarrels among scholars as to whether the Beatrice of the *Vita* was an actual historical person, since the young woman can so easily be interpreted in terms of various abstractions. Did the Beatrice of the *Vita* have any actual Florentine counterpart? The answer is Yes, but the tendency to allegorize her out of existence is not unfounded. That in turn may suggest that the Mary of Dante's great poem is also a pardonable poetic exaggeration, a Florentine excess. It would be a profound mistake to think so.

The Blessed Virgin of the *Comedy* is the Blessed Virgin of Christian faith. One of the unfortunate and doubtless unintended effects of the Reformation has been to create among many believers suspicion as to Mary's role in the plan of salvation. What need have we for any mediator but Christ himself? Devotion to Mary is thought to intrude between the soul and God, or to divert the soul in its journey to God. It is a commonplace that many converts found the Catholic emphasis on Mary a great obstacle to be overcome. John Henry Newman—I am tempted to say, even John Henry Newman—felt this for a time.

Dante has softened this suspicion for many, enabling them to regard Mary as a character in a poem so that disbelief could be suspended for the nonce. But the Mary of the poem never speaks except in words taken from the Gospels, and she is no more an invention or a mere device than are Hell and Purgatory and Heaven. Whatever Dante says of her is grounded in Scripture, the Church fathers, the great doctors of the Church in the Middle Ages, and in the liturgy, art, and music of the Church. If that doctrine, that Mariology, has been lost or attenuated for us, Dante provides a powerful means of recovering it. Any reader who has fears to be allayed should consider these words of St. Bernard of Clairvaux: "There is no doubt that whatever we offer in praise of the Mother, pertains to the Son; and, when we honor the Son, we do not take away from the glory of the Mother. For if, *The wise son is the glory of the father*, as Solomon says, how much more glorious does that make the mother of Wisdom?"[3]

Incipit Vita Nova

If we know nothing else about Dante, we know him as the author of the *Divine Comedy*. This great poem, however, is the culmination of a writing career that began with lyric poems in the Provençal or troubador tradition. In the *Vita Nuova*, he gathers some of those poems into an account that is deceptively simple—on the surface.

It is not uncommon for a poet, particularly a lyric poet, to make himself the subject of his poetry. Nonetheless, any reader will be initially struck by the confidence with which Dante regards himself as a mirror of the human condition. His life is not a random sequence of events but an intelligible story with a beginning, a middle, and an end.

That Dante draws selectively on his memory is clear from the opening lines of the *Vita Nuova*. The memories to be recalled are governed by the event when "a new life begins" (*Incipit Vita Nova*), the Latin rubric under which the book is written and which provides the title (in Italian, *Vita Nuova*) of the little book. It is an ingenious interplay of prose and verse. The poems may have antedated the composition of the book, but they are so deftly folded into the narrative as to make a whole, and we are invited to take the poems as contemporary comments on the prosaic events.

The structure of the book can be discerned in the arrangement of the poems on which Dante, remembering, comments. Dante is at once a personage in the narrative and the narrator; as the latter, he seeks the meaning of his love for Beatrice. Of the thirty-one poems that alternate with prose, thirty are either sonnets or odes (*canzoni*) and one is a ballad. Their arrangement is not random, and the prose sections underscore this fact.

The opening paragraph, later referred to as the prologue, is this:

> In quella parte del libro della mia memoria dinanzi alla quale poco si potrebbe leggere, si trova una rubrica la quale dice *Incipit Vita Nova.* Sotto la quale rubrica io trovo scripte le parole le quali è mio intendimento d'asemplare in questo libello, e se non tutte, almeno la loro sententia. (*VN* 1.1)

> In the part of the book of my memory before which there is little legible there is a rubric which says, A New Life Begins. Under this rubric I find written words whose meaning it is my intention to set forth in this little book, if not all of them, at least their substance.

The next sentence begins with *nove,* nine, the number that is "friendly to Beatrice" and whose function is far more theological than numerological. Nine = 3 × 3, and 3 is the number of the Trinity. The prominence of nine is clear in the opening chapter, which tells of the author's first meeting with Beatrice. It is the basis of Dante's calling Beatrice a miracle.

Dante's story in the opening chapter is well known. At the age of nine, he sees Beatrice (*la gloriosa donna de la mia mente*) for the first time, herself just beginning her ninth year. She is humble and honest, dressed as befits her age, and of course, beautiful (although, as has been pointed out, Dante never calls her beautiful in the physical sense: his infatuation, his love, goes deeper than that). His reaction is seismic.[4] He trembles, he is shaken, and he switches to Latin: "Ecce

Deus fortior me, qui veniens dominabitur michi!" (Behold, here is a god stronger than I who is coming to dominate me!).

The occurrence of occasional Latin sentences among the Italian is significant. First was *Incipit Vita Nova* and then the "Ecce Deus," quickly followed by "Apparuit iam beatitudo vestra!" (Now appears your beatitude!) and "Heu miser, quia frequenter impeditus ero deinceps!" (Alas, how often I will be disturbed from now on!). It is as if these Latin sentences govern the Italian narrative; their meaning is of heightened importance. That Beatrice's name is linked with beatitude, happiness, is underscored by the Latin *beatitudo*. She did not seem to be the daughter of a mortal man, but of a god, Dante remarks, quoting Homer. As a mere boy, he sought out occasions when he might catch a glimpse of her. After telling us this, he states that he will not dwell on it because it might seem an exercise in fiction to ascribe such passions and actions to one so young. He will go on to what, in the book of memory, comes under more important headings. But first he makes clear that his love for Beatrice is not merely a thing of the passions; that love is always under the counsel and aegis of reason. That is, his feelings are governed by intelligence, not vice versa.

Nine years after the first encounter with Beatrice he sees her again, clothed all in white and accompanied by two older ladies. She looks at him and greets him with indescribable courtesy, "which is now rewarded in a greater sphere." This is our first overt clue that at the time of writing, Beatrice is already dead,[5] and thus there is narrative tension between what Dante the narrator knows and what the Dante who figures in the narration knows. It happened that it was the ninth hour of the day when Beatrice looked at him so tenderly.

After this meeting and greeting, Dante, inebriated by the sweetness of her voice, repairs to his room where, in his sleep, he has a vision. An imposing figure appears, and of the many things he says, Dante recalls only "Ego dominus tuus" (I am thy God). The figure is the god of love, and he holds in his arms the sleeping figure of Beatrice, covered with a crimson cloth. The god also holds in his hand a fiery object and says to Beatrice, "Vide cor tuum." Beatrice awakens, and the god has her eat Dante's heart. Whereupon the god, grieving, ascends with the lady to heaven. On waking, Dante realizes that all this has occurred in the fourth hour of the night, that is, the first of the nine last hours of night. And then follows the first sonnet of the *Vita Nuova*, which Dante intends to show to his fellow poets, among them certainly his good friend Guido Cavalcanti:

> A ciascun'alma presa e gentil core
> nel cui cospecto ven lo dir presente,
> in ciò che mi riscriva 'n suo parvente,
> salute in lor segnor, cioè Amore.
> Già eran quasi che alterzate l'ore
> del tempo che omne stella n'è lucente,
> quando m'apparve Amor subitamente,
> cui essenza membrar mi dà orrore.
>   Allegro mi sembrava Amor tenendo
> meo core in mano, e nelle braccia avea
> madonna involta in un drappo dormendo.
>   Poi la svegliava, e d'esto core ardendo
> lei paventosa umilmente pascea.
> Apresso gir lo ne vedea piangendo.
>
> (*VN* 1.21–23)

In Dante Gabriel Rossetti's translation,

> To every heart which the sweet pain doth move,
>   And unto which these words may now be brought
>   For true interpretation and kind thought,
>   Be greeting in our Lord's name, which is Love.
> Of those long hours wherein the stars, above,
>   Wake and keep watch, the third was almost nought
>   When Love was shown me with such terrors fraught
>   As may not carelessly be spoke of.
>
> He seemed like one who is full of joy, and had
>   My heart within his hand, and on his arm
>   My lady, with a mantle round her, slept;
> Whom (having waken'd her) anon he made
>   To eat that heart; she ate, as fearing harm.
>   Then he went out; and as he went, he wept.[6]

We notice that the sonnet does not mention the god ascending toward heaven with Beatrice. At the time it was written, Dante did not realize the role his beloved was to play in the *Comedy*. His poem, like those of the poets whose thoughts on it he solicits, is written within the bounds of courtly love. And he reports that Guido's reply, in a sonnet of his own, seals their friendship.

As the narrative continues, the conventions of such verse continue. Dante finds himself in a room with Beatrice. When he gazes at her, another woman is in his line of sight, which misleads others as to the object of his affection. This screen lady, as she is called (Dante refers to her as a "screen to the truth"), will play her role for a time, enabling Dante to conceal that the true object of his love is Beatrice. Meanwhile, he composes a list of sixty women and, *mirabile dictu*, Beatrice's name is ninth on the list. Then the screen lady leaves town and Dante writes a sonnet, seemingly addressed to her, but in truth addressed to Beatrice.

This sonnet begins in a way that must capture our attention: "O voi che per la via d'Amor passate, / attendete e guardate / s'elli è dolore alcun, quanto 'l mio, grave" (O all ye who pass by the way of Love, look and see if there is any sorrow like unto mine). Lest we fail to recognize the allusion, Dante, in the prose explanation of the sonnet, directs us to the Prophet Jeremiah: "O vos omnes qui transitis per viam, attendite et videte si est dolor sicut dolor meus" (O all ye who pass by the way, look and see if there is any sorrow like unto mine). Did the poet, when he wrote these words, simply pick them up from the Christian ambience and forget to what liturgical purpose they had been put? In the *Vita Nuova* he makes the biblical reference clear but not its application. These words of Jeremiah are attributed in the Catholic liturgy to the Blessed Virgin, the *Mater Dolorosa*, when she meets Jesus carrying his cross to Golgotha. Doubtless the reader is meant to remember this liturgical use, and it is an indication of the significance to Dante of the life and death of Beatrice.

As with certain descriptions of Beatrice, the reader is likely to feel uneasiness at the way in which this originally childish love becomes, in Dante's recall, intertwined with references to Christ and to Mary. The account is posthumous, Beatrice is dead when it is written, but before her actual death in the narrative, Dante will dream it, will see her on her deathbed, and when she dies will describe its cosmic effect by appeal to what happened when Our Lord died on the cross. And the lady of a friend in the *Vita Nuova*—her name is Giovanna—will be compared to John the Baptist, the voice crying in the wilderness, calling for repentance and preparing for the coming of the Messiah. Scholars call attention to the biblical echoes.[7]

Few figures from the Gospel accounts impress themselves on the believer's mind and imagination more than the son of Mary's cousin Elizabeth, namely, John the Baptist. A surprising number of direct quotations from John are given us in the Gospels, and to the present day they have captivated writers, not least Albert Camus, whose judge penitent is named Jean-Baptiste Clamant. John the Baptist is a *vox clamantis*, a voice crying in the wilderness. Is the evocation by Dante merely a similar literary use? Or does it cut deeper than that?

What are we to make of the *Vita Nuova*? It is a love story, of course, but one which, in the manner of courtly love, seems to float free of possession. The actual Beatrice eventually married, but her husband is as unimportant to Dante as Daisy Buchanan's was to Gatsby. (For that matter, Gemma, Dante's wife, never makes it onto the page.)[8] From the outset, the love that is celebrated is remarkably asexual. That could be accounted for by the troubador tradition. The woman stirs the imagination and devotion of the man; she is seen as the embodiment of beauty, physical and spiritual. The flesh and blood woman is so transmuted by this intense sublimation that she can seem hardly more than an occasion for the poet to celebrate her. In Dante's case, however, the sublimation echoes with scriptural allusions; the religious meaning is essential.

Beatrice is presented as having a profound devotion to the Blessed Virgin, so much so that after her death Dante thinks of her as enthroned in heaven with Mary: "quando lo Signore della iusti-tia chiamòe questa gentilissima a gloriare sotto la 'nsegna di quella Regina benedecta Maria, lo cui nome fue in grandissima reverenzia nelle parole di questa Beatrice beata" (when the Lord of Justice called this most gentle one to glory under the ensign of Mary that blessed Queen, whose name was ever spoken with the greatest reverence by that blessed Beatrice [*VN* 19.1]). Dante's reader grows accustomed to his way of intermingling the sacred and profane, the physical and spiritual, the temporal and eternal. We are not surprised that eventually he will find a kindred spirit in Bernard of Clairvaux, the austere yet passionate Cistercian, whose love for Mary may seem to the cynical the compensation of the celibate.

The *Vita Nuova* is saturated with theological references. Our rather limited interest in it is the role Mary plays in this early work. The new life would seem to be the result of a conversion—you shall have life, and that more abundantly. The role of Beatrice, at first the object of a young boy's infatuation, evolves into a salvific one. She is Dante's beatitude, the means of his turning to a concern for his eternal beatitude. Some scholars have stressed this evolution in terms of Dante's changing understanding of his purpose as a poet. In the troubador tradition, the beloved is the cause of pain. More importantly, as Charles Singleton has pointed out, the beloved seems an alternative to the lover's true good.[9] Many troubadors ended their lives in monasteries, doing penance, as it were, for the loves they had celebrated. One is reminded of Chaucer's Retractions in his *Canterbury Tales*, in which he expresses remorse that his works may have been occasions of sin to his readers.[10] But the troubadors were remorseful for their deviation from the true object of love, God. Singleton claims that Dante's great achievement is to have recognized the rivalry of loves and to have solved it. When Dante turns to God, Beatrice remains. She is not an impediment; she is the facilitator of his salvation.

The device of the "screen lady" in the *Vita Nuova* suggests a daring hypothesis. If another lady could provide the means of concealing Dante's true love, could it be that Beatrice herself is something of a screen lady? Beatrice's devotion to Mary and the description of her ascension into heaven at her death calls to mind Our Lady's assumption into heaven.[11] As Guglielmo Gorni writes, "From her birth Beatrice was destined for heaven, precociously summoned to 'glory under the ensign of Mary that blessed Queen.'"[12] And to Beatrice is applied the attribute *par excellence* of Mary, that is, *gratia plena*, full of grace. As Gorni also observes, "It is without doubt that in the *Vita Nuova* the similarity to Mary works in tandem with that of Beatrice as figure of Christ."[13]

Thus, without in any way calling into question the historical reality of Beatrice, we find in the *Vita Nuova* a progressive understanding of the role she plays for Dante. Things said about her make it clear that she is a figure both of Christ and of Mary. In that sense, it does not seem fanciful to think of her as a screen lady. At the end of the *Vita*, Dante realizes that he must now speak of her in quite a different way than he had in the earlier poems that the little book incorporates. His understanding of the kind of poet he must become is integral to this realization. He will become a theological poet.

In keeping with the interpretation that Dante now views himself as a new kind of poet, the *Vita Nuova* ends with a memorable resolution. Dante is dissatisfied with what he has accomplished. He longs to celebrate his love for Beatrice more adequately, but in order to do that a good deal more is required of him. After the last sonnet he writes:

> Apresso questo sonetto apparve a me una mirabile visione, nella quale io vidi cose che mi fecero proporre di non dire più di questa benedecta infino a tanto che io potessi più degnamente tractare di lei. E di venire a ciò io studio quanto posso, sì com'ella sae, veracemente. Sì che, se piacere sarà di Colui a cui tutte le cose vivono, che la mia vita duri per alquanti anni, io spero di dire di lei quello che mai non fue detto d'alcuna. E poi piaccia a colui che è sire della cortesia che la mia anima sen possa gire a vedere la gloria della sua donna, cioè di quella benedecta Beatrice, la quale gloriosamente mira nella faccia di Colui "qui est per omnia secula benedictus." (*VN* 31)

> After this sonnet a wonderful vision came to me, in which I saw things which caused me to resolve to say nothing further of this blessed one in order that I might more worthily treat of her. To that end, I study as much as possible, as she truly knows. Accordingly, should it please Him by whom all things live that my life endure for some years, I hope to say of her what has never been said of any woman. May it then be pleasing to Him who is Lord of courtesy that my soul may go and see the glory of that lady, that is of the blessed Beatrice, who looks gloriously on the face of Him who is forever and ever blessed.

Who will not see in this promissory note the intention to write the *Commedia*? Alas, matters are blurred by the fact that Dante's next major work was the *Convivio*, not the *Commedia*. In the *Convivio* we are told that Dante has devoted himself to thirty months of study in the religious houses of Florence, that is, in the house of study of the Franciscans, Santa Croce, and that of the Dominicans, Santa Maria Novella.[14] The *Convivio* as we have it is a large work, and if its plan had been carried to completion, it would have been massive. But it was left incomplete. Why?

Dante in the *Convivio* had set himself the task of putting into the vernacular language the Latin learning he had acquired in the schools of philosophy and theology, to make it accessible to non-scholars, both in prose and poetry. We notice that he assumes the role of mediator between the learned and simple. The *Convivio*, however, does not wear its learning lightly. Did Dante come to doubt the effectiveness of what he was writing? Did he repent of portraying himself as one who had transcended his love for Beatrice in order to devote himself to philosophy and theology? Did he remember the resolution with which the *Vita Nuova* ends and conceive a more effective way of fulfilling it, a way that would eschew prose and rely on poetry alone? This is speculative, to be sure, but so are all other accounts of why the *Convivio* was left unfinished. In any case, the idea of the *Commedia* was born. The intention to speak of Beatrice as no woman has ever been spoken of before returned. Dante had prayed for time to fulfill that intention. His prayer was answered. The result was the most magnificent poem ever written, one with immediate charm for any reader but also one replete with allusions to the knowledge he had gained, and with lore to keep scholars busy. The sheer bulk of Dante studies make it impossible for anyone to profit from more than a fraction of them.

Conscious of the difficulties of the task, let us now follow the thread that binds it all together, the role of the Blessed Virgin in Dante's life and in the poem.

TWO

In the Midst of My Days

I said: In the midst of my days I shall go to the gates of hell.
I sought for the residue of my years.

—Isa. 38:10

Nel mezzo del cammin: Midway this way

The *Commedia* is divided into three parts, each called a "cantica"—
Hell, Purgatory, and Paradise—and contains a total of one hundred
cantos. The second and third parts have precisely thirty-three cantos
each; the first has the extra canto. The first canto of the first cantica is
a prologue to the entire poem. It begins thus:

> Nel mezzo del cammin di nostra vita
> mi ritrovai per una selva oscura,
> che la diritta via era smarrita.
> *(Inf. 1.1–3)*

Dorothy Sayers has translated this as well as anyone and better than
some (save perhaps for the rendering of *smarrita*) as:

> Midway this way of life we're bound upon,
>> I woke to find myself in a dark wood,
>> Where the right road was wholly lost and gone.[1]

There is not a line of Dante, indeed scarcely a word of his, that has not been subjected to scholarly analysis and thereby generated some measure of division of opinion.[2] Obviously, if the only way to an understanding of the poem lay through the thicket of that scholarship, we would be in a dark wood indeed, if not wholly lost and gone. Scholarship and criticism are lovely things, so long as they bring us back to what they study and criticize and do not substitute for it. Dante scholarship, to the modest degree that I know it, is remarkably free of the pedantry that is the death of learning.[3] Dantisti, as they are called, have by and large retained some measure of the wonder and excitement of their first encounter with the poem. Needless to say, all of us must first encounter the poem, read the *Commedia*, before commentaries on it can make sense. Even in that first reading we will be grateful for the notes in the edition with which we happen to begin. Even readers for whom Italian is their mother tongue need such notes.

Who cannot catch the literal sense of that opening tercet? Someone is speaking to us in the first person, telling us he woke up lost in a dark wood. He is recalling his past and presuming our interest. And he has it. It's a great opening. One gets used to admiring Dante's skill, but of course one is simply calling attention to his own keen discernment.

It being clear, then, that the opening lines of the *Commedia* speak immediately to a first reader, we are better prepared to see what scholars can do to enhance our rereading. A rule of thumb for literature, C. S. Lewis suggested, is that it is something we reread.[4] There are stories and poems we read once and that's that. They have given us all they have. The things we go back to again and again are rich with levels not apparent at first blush. In rereading we notice things we didn't notice before, and this deepens our appreciation. A critic such as G. K. Chesterton brings us back to Chaucer or Dickens with more sensitive antennae, and this heightens our enjoyment. In his *Book of Problems*, Aristotle asked, twice, why do we like the old songs best? It is not true that familiarity always breeds contempt: there could be no happy families if it were. "Shall I compare thee to a summer's day?" Not on the first date, certainly, or not in the first moment of being smitten. The comparison rides on, depends upon, loving the other person as she or he is. (Though, as W. B. Yeats said of Lady Ann Gregory, "Only God could love you for yourself alone, and not your yellow hair.") So too, any poem engages us first and then invites reflection. In the case of Dante, that simple truth is not merely instantiated, it is required.

The Bible, Old and New Testaments, is read by or to the faithful and, having been read, is analyzed in the homily. Believers reflect on Holy Writ in the awareness that it is the Word of God speaking to us in our own tongues. In the *De doctrina christiana*, St. Augustine gives his account of the multiple senses of Scripture, the layers of meaning in the sacred text. In the *Summa theologiae*, St. Thomas Aquinas asks whether Sacred Scripture has senses beyond the literal and replies:

> It should be noticed that the author of Sacred Scripture is God in whose power it is not only to make vocal sounds have meanings (even men can bring this about) but also that the things themselves should mean. While it is true that in any science, words have meanings, it is proper to this science that the things signified by the words also signify something. The first meaning, whereby words signify things, is the primary sense, the historical or literal sense. But the meaning whereby the things signified by the words signify other things, is called the spiritual sense, which is grounded in the literal and presupposes it. (*ST* Ia, q. 1, a. 10)

According to Thomas, this further, spiritual sense has been given various subdivisions. He himself divides the spiritual sense into the allegorical, the moral, and the anagogical senses. The allegorical sense is exemplified in the way in which events in the Old Testament are figures of the New Law. The moral sense is exemplified in the way in which Christ's words and actions, and what is said of Him, are signs of what we ought to do. The anagogical sense points to eternal glory. That the literal sense should be pregnant with these various spiritual senses is attributed to God, who is the author of Sacred Scripture. So what has all this to do with reading Dante?

Literary criticism has been called a secular form of biblical criticism. Whatever truth there may be in this generalization, it is necessarily true of Dante scholarship. In his letter to Can Grande della Scala, dedicating the third cantica to this patron, Dante refers to the *Commedia* as a whole and gives instructions on how to read it.

Dantisti differ as to the authenticity of this letter—the thirteenth and last of Dante's Latin epistles that we have—but such disputes could scarcely interest us if we had not read it. Let us imagine ourselves looking over the shoulder of its addressee, the imperial vicar and lord of Verona, and let us take it to be from Dante.[5] It begins with an unctuously laudatory description of Can Grande and the memorable self-description, "Dantes Alagherii, florentinus natione non moribus" (Dante Alighieri, Florentine in nation but not in morals). Praise of Can Grande continues through the first four paragraphs, followed by the author's discussion of his great poem.

He begins with a citation from a Latin translation of Aristotle's *Metaphysics*, Book 2: "sicut res se habet ad esse, sic se habet ad veritatem" (the truth of things follows on the kind of being they have). There are things that are what they are and yet are also related to other things, as one who is a man may also be a father or son. The implication seems to be that since the great poem is related to the author, its truth must be sought in that relationship. This is a rather ponderous way of saying that it is to the author we should go to find out what the poem is about. Dante then invokes a device devised by commentators on classical works, namely, the prologue that precedes the analysis of the text. There are six things that a commentator should do before beginning his chief work; he should tell us what the subject of the work is, who wrote it, its form, its end, its title, and to what part of philosophy it belongs.

A first thing to notice about this is Dante's unblushing application to his own work of a requirement to be met by commentaries on acknowledged classics. There is a modest foreshadowing of this in the *Vita Nuova* in the didactic discussions that follow the poems. Dante was probably acquainted with the requirements of a prologue from reading Boethius, or Thomas Aquinas commenting on Aristotle. Dante's practice in the *Vita Nuova* might be said to have a precedent in Boethius's *Consolation of Philosophy*, that death-row classic which also alternates poetry and prose. But surely to apply to his own work the conventions of the classical commentary is somewhat astonishing. It tells us at least two things. First, Dante had no doubt of the importance of what he had accomplished. Second, he believes that his great poem is as well-thought-out as any classical treatise and can thus sustain, even invite, close scrutiny.

This initial astonishment is soon followed by another greater one. Dante applies to the *Commedia* the techniques of biblical interpretation:

> It should be known that this work has not only a simple sense, indeed it can be called polysemous, that is, of several senses; for the first sense is had in the letter and another is given through what is signified literally. The first sense is called the literal, the second allegorical, or moral, or anagogical. (*Ep.* 13.7)

Lest we miss the parallel, Dante goes on to illustrate these various senses by analyzing two verses of Scripture: "When Israel went out of Egypt, the house of Jacob from a barbarous people, Juda was made his sanctuary, Israel his kingdom" (Ps. 113[114]:1–2).

If we take only the literal meaning of this passage, it tells us of the exodus from Egypt of the sons of Israel at the time of Moses. But if we take it allegorically, it refers to our redemption by Christ; its moral sense tells us of the conversion of our souls from the grief and misery of sin to the state of grace; and its anagogical sense tells us of the exit of the saintly soul from the slavery of this corrupt world to the freedom of eternal glory. Dante adds that all of these mystical senses can be gathered under the appellation *allegorical* in that they are another (*alleon*) sense that differs from the historical or literal sense.

With that in hand, Dante turns to the *Commedia* and indicates its various senses. Literally, it concerns simply the state of souls after death, for on this topic the whole work turns. However, taken allegorically, its subject is man insofar as by the merit or demerit consequent upon his free actions he is eternally and justly rewarded or punished. The poem will show us souls after death and make clear how their condition, whether of weal or woe, was freely and justly achieved.

This application of the senses of Scripture to the *Commedia* poses problems, to which Dante refers elsewhere.[6] The obvious difficulty arises from the way St. Thomas spoke of those further senses of Scripture—the way the things meant by the words can mean yet other things—as something of which only God, not man, is capable. After all, He is the creator of things. A preliminary resolution of this difficulty for Dante might be sought in the fact that the story of the *Commedia* is essentially the story of Scripture, that is, the story of salvation or damnation. The characters and episodes put before us may not be biblical, but the allegorical meaning of the poem is. This is clear from the fact that the allegorical sense that chiefly interests Dante is the moral.

Continuing with the classical demands of a prologue, he asks to which part of philosophy the *Commedia* falls. We will waive for the moment any discussion of the special problem posed by the philosophical or theological poet. Surely poetry is one thing and philosophy another; a fortiori, theology differs from poetry. But it would be premature to consider this difficulty now. The answer Dante gives is that the *Commedia* falls to moral philosophy. That follows from his announced end or purpose of the work: "The point of the work in whole and in part is to move those living in this life from a state of misery and lead them to a state of happiness" (*Ep.* 13.15).

One further question from the letter to Can Grande: Why is the poem called a comedy? Dante's answer presupposes that tragedy ends in bitter defeat, whereas comedy has a happy ending. "And thus it is clear why the present work is called the Comedy. For if we look to the matter, from a horrible and fetid beginning, which is Hell, it moves in the end to the desirable and gracious Paradise" (*Ep.* 13.10).

La diritta via: The narrow way

At the opening of the *Inferno* we found Dante lost in a dark wood at midlife. What is midlife? "The sum of our years is seventy, and if we are strong, eighty" (Ps. 89[90]:10). The authoritative biblical span being seventy years, the Dante of the poem is at the halfway point of thirty-five.[7] Of course, there is optimism in this; Dante did not live to see his seventieth year. But he is not predicting so much as applying to himself the well-known biblical text. He was born in 1265, his life overlapping those of Thomas Aquinas and Bonaventure—both of whom died in 1274—for nine years. That makes the year of the poem 1300, the year of the first Jubilee, called by Pope Boniface VIII, when the faithful made a pilgrimage to Rome to visit the great churches and to see such marvels as the Veil of Veronica. (Dante alludes to this veil in the *Vita Nuova*, and later, in the *Comedy*, he describes a pilgrim come from afar, perhaps Croatia, whose lifelong hope is realized when he sees the veil on which is imprinted the bloody face of Christ.)

Not only is the poem set in 1300, it begins in Holy Week on Good Friday and proceeds through Easter, until in the *Paradiso* such temporal references drop away. By some calculations, the activities of the *Inferno* are covered in a single day. Jubilee signifies a call for repentance and atonement, Holy Week the passion and death of Christ that won our salvation, and Easter the hope of our own resurrection and eternal bliss. It is helpful, though not immediately necessary, to know this in order to grasp the sense of the dark wood in which Dante has awakened.

He is filled with fear by his surroundings and doubts that he has words to describe it; the mere memory of it is bad enough. How did he get there? He cannot say, so weary was he when he wandered from the true path, *la verace via*. He is in a valley, a forbidding hill looms, but a glimpse of sun causes him to take heart. And then he is suddenly assailed by three beasts. First a leopard comes and stands athwart his path; it is described in pleasing detail. Then comes another beast, a lion, soon to be joined by a wolf.

The obvious sense of this encounter is that Dante, having wandered from the right path, is prevented from finding his way by the appearance of these wild beasts. Even on a first reading we pick up clues that Dante's plight carries meanings beyond the surface sense. What is the right path (*la diritta via*), and what is the relevance of being thirty-five to someone lost in the woods? The occurrence of both "our" (*nostra*) and "me" (*mi*) in those first lines draw us into the scene, suggesting that Dante's situation is at once his and very likely ours. Halfway through the journey we all make, he finds himself lost. The suggestion is that we are all on the way, pilgrims, and that life itself is aimed at something. The end is death, certainly, but death is not a destination so much as an ending. St. Thomas, in his commentary on verses 5–6 of the Second Epistle to the Corinthians, where Paul is speaking of the reward awaiting the faithful after death, provides us with the assumption behind the scene: "In the present life man is as it were on a kind of journey, because he ought to aim at heaven."[8]

The right path is the one that will take us beyond death to heaven. We are willy-nilly mortal, but our eternal post-mortem condition is up to us. Having read the letter to Can Grande, we know that Dante's aim in his great poem is to lead us from the misery and sin of our present life into the glory and happiness of eternal life. When Thornton Wilder gave one of his novels the title *Heaven's My Destination*, he was plucking a phrase from a little jingle kids wrote in the front of their schoolbooks, an evocation of childlike faith.[9] There was nothing ironic in that choice. Wilder's readers, not so long ago, would have responded to the title as to a truism.[10] Dante's contemporary readers would have found the allegorical meaning of the *Commedia* as familiar as the literal. Of course, the literal meaning of the poem—heaven or hell—already invokes religious belief. It is the detail and imagery of the afterlife, not the fact of it, that enriches the allegorical meaning of the poem. That we are all pilgrims, something brought home in a special way during a Jubilee year, would be a commonplace to Dante's readers. The Dante of the poem is a particular Florentine with his quite definite life story and also, in a way, all of us.

Most of us have seen enough MGM movies to be acquainted with the phrase *ars gratia artis*—art for art's sake—and whatever we think of its use as a motto for the run-of-the-mill film, we have probably some sense of its meaning. "A poem should not mean / But be," we might remember, waiving the inanity of this phrase from Archibald MacLeish's "Ars poetica." Isn't Dante's stated intention in writing the *Commedia* a culpable confusion of genera? Edifying discourses are one thing, but surely poetry is something else. Whoever thought that the poetry, the music, the drama, and the novels we enjoy have anything to do with the moral, let alone the religious, life? The answer is, just about everybody until a short time ago and many writers and readers still.

Flannery O'Connor, calling herself a hillbilly Thomist who read a little bit of the *Summa theologiae* every day, said that all literature is anagogical. All! Perhaps she had in mind that passage from the

Summa which explains the senses of Scripture. Did she mean that all literature is ethical or religious?

Well, what is a story? Any story begins with a protagonist confronting a dilemma that must be resolved, a problem, a crossroads. And he or she must act. This protagonist will have a name, sometimes the name of an historical character, but we will ask for more from a story than we would from history. The protagonist's efforts to resolve the dilemma, to solve the problem, to take one road rather than another, will encounter difficulties that he must overcome. They may overcome him, or a first attempt may simply worsen his situation. But he goes on. A story might give us a hero whose efforts take him more and more deeply into trouble until a dark moment is reached when it looks as if all is lost. Then, by his own efforts, and plausibly, he sees a way out, takes it, and the problem with which he began is solved. End of story.

This is more or less what we find in the *Poetics* of Aristotle. Why are we interested in the activities of imaginary characters or the imaginary activities of historical characters—of Hamlet, David Copperfield, Becky Sharpe, the warden in Trollope, Jay Gatsby, Huckleberry Finn, Caesar and Cleopatra, Richard II, and on and on, to invoke stories we read again and again? Imaginary frogs in real gardens, or real frogs in imaginary gardens? In real life we rarely find the economy of action that characterizes fiction. A story concentrates the mind and imagination; the events have a beginning, a middle, and an end, which confers a meaning on them. The end could be death or marriage or finding El Dorado or nailing Al Capone for income tax evasion or any number of things, but it is a solution that focuses the account of someone addressing a problem.

We become involved in stories because their characters are in some way ourselves. They are our better or worse selves, but not too much the one or the other. We follow an imagined version of the choices that make up any human life, choices that matter. We are what we do, and characters in a story reveal who they are by their actions and choices. In real life, bounders succeed and the innocent suffer; they do in fiction, too, but the story makes sense of that in a way real life seldom does. Any story worth reading again will tell us something about the human condition we recognize as true. There is something of Macbeth or Lady Macbeth in each of us, something of Lord Jim, and something of Dante.

It matters what we read and enjoy. If we did not think the young are better for reading Shakespeare and F. Scott Fitzgerald or J. D. Salinger, why have millions of students been assigned *Hamlet*, *The Great Gatsby*, or *Catcher in the Rye*? But better in what way? Cardinal Newman, in "The Tamworth Reading Room," made gentle fun of those who thought that providing books for the masses would have some kind of automatic effect in changing their lives for the better. We could substitute the aim of the Carnegie Public Libraries or the silly assumption of Ray Bradbury's *Fahrenheit 451* that anything printed is sacred. Surely it would be excessive to think that being able to appreciate *Lord Jim* would make the reader brave. And we mustn't forget Don Quixote, the character not the book.

If literature has a moral effect, it is more subtle than that. But, as Delmore Schwartz put it, "In dreams begin responsibilities." The ideals and the models of action with which our reading furnishes the mind and imagination provide a deep background for who we want to be or want not to be. Of course it is silly to think that literature will make us what we ought to be. Does it differ from moral philosophy in that? Aristotle said that no one becomes good by studying moral philosophy. Yet the only reason for studying it is that we might become better. Aristotle's point was that knowing what to do is not tantamount to doing it. Moral philosophy, however, is less efficacious than literature, not the other way around. Becoming the Archbishop of Sante Fe as we read Willa Cather's *Death Comes for the Archbishop* engages us more completely than reading about states of life in the *Summa theologiae*.

When Dante tells us that the *Commedia* is meant to lead us from the misery of sin to the happiness of heaven, we can be sure that he has at least as keen a sense as do we of the distance between his poem and any conversion of ours. But distance does not mean irrelevance.

The leopard, the lion, and the wolf

The beasts that menace Dante in the first canto of the *Commedia* stand for something. What? A good and common guess is Lust, Pride, and

Avarice. Since the first canto is a prologue to the entire poem, we will meet these beasts again, the beasts within us: "all that is in the world is the lust of the flesh, and the lust of the eyes, and the pride of life" (1 John 2:16). "I am a little world made cunningly / Of elements, and an Angelike spright," wrote John Donne,[11] but the earliest reflections on human life take into account this division within ourselves. The good that we would, we do not; the evil that we would not do, that we do. We find the thought in Ovid as well as in St. Paul. Plato told a story in the *Republic* of the soul's being incarcerated in the body and thus losing the knowledge that it previously had of reality. We find ourselves prisoners in a cave, mistaking shadows and images for their real counterparts. Liberation from the cave may seem to be simply a matter of gaining knowledge, but Plato knows that we have become affectively attached to shadows and images. The task of philosophy is to alter our affections as well as to change our minds, and to do the one in order that the other might be brought about. In the words chosen by Cardinal Newman for his tomb, *Ex umbris et imaginibus ad veritatem:* Out of shadows and phantasms into the truth.

Why do we sin against the light of reason and fail to do what we know is the good and fulfilling thing? Well, for one thing, we have appetites other than will, or the rational appetite, and those lower appetites can cloud the mind when we act. The immediate pleasurable good to which we have become attached trumps the good recognized by mind as our true good.

Dante, like Aristotle, did not think that evil was some *thing* that attracts us. Only the good attracts; that is what we mean by good. Evil as such repels, just as, on the level of sense, pain repels whereas pleasure attracts. It is because there are goods and goods that we can act defectively. A pleasure of the senses is a good, and we do not decide to be drawn to it; it is natural that we should be so drawn. No more do we decide to shrink from the prospect of pain. These affective responses, these natural appetites, do not of themselves propel us to one course of action rather than another. All of us feel fear at the prospect of bodily harm and death, but the brave person behaves one way and the coward another. Kierkegaard's aesthete, in his *Either/Or,* as well as all of us in certain moods, imagines a mindless pursuit of pleasure, self-contained and untrammeled by an antecedent warning or subsequent remorse. This could only come about if we had natural appetites and nothing more—that is, if we were mere animals. But we have minds as well. "Are passions then the pagans of the soul, reason alone baptized?" This is the question, taken from the English poet Edward Young, that is the motto of Kierkegaard's *Either/Or*.

Only the good can attract us, but some goods are merely the satisfaction of hunger or thirst or the sexual drive. If these desires were all we were, there would be no moral task. The moral task is to integrate the pursuit of these goods into the overall good of the acting person. The beasts in the first canto can be taken to stand for our natural appetites. If the pursuit of these is not subordinate to the judgment of reason, it is disordered. That is what moral evil is, the disordered pursuit of a good. That is what has taken Dante from the true path and brought him into a dark wood, into the misery of sin. And we all know what that's like.

The precise correlation of the three beasts with particular natural appetites in Dante is not easy. Sometimes the leopard is interpreted as lust, sometimes avarice. Efforts have been made to employ the Aristotelian division of incontinence, malice, and bestiality to identify the beasts as providing the rationale for the three main circles of hell. There are political interpretations as well—the leopard is Florence, the lion the king of France, and the wolf the Roman curia. That wider possible significance underscores an important fact. Although Dante finds himself alone in the dark wood, he is not the autonomous individual of recent moral theory. For one thing, he is a Florentine, citizen of a particular city and member of a definite family. One doesn't get into moral trouble in isolation; one cannot get out of it alone. We are by nature social and political animals.

Mio maestro e 'l mio autore: My master, my author

A figure appears, and Dante appeals to him for help. "Have mercy on me," Dante cries, "be ye man or a shade of man." The figure answers, 'I am no man, though man I was, my parents were from Lombardy and both from the country of Mantua.'" *Mantua me genuit.* Born during

the reign of Caesar, he flourished under Augustus in a time of false
and lying gods.

> Poeta fui, e cantai di quel giusto
> figliuol d'Anchise che venne da Troia,
> poi che 'l superbo Ilïón fu combusto.
> (*Inf.* 1.73–75)

"I was a poet, and sang of that upright son of Anchises who came
from Troy after the burning of that pride of Ilion." The figure is Virgil, the poet of the *Aeneid*, the great epic that tells of the founding of
Rome. Dante is overwhelmed.

> Tu se' lo mio maestro et 'l mio autore,
> tu se' solo colui da cu' io tolsi
> lo bello stilo che m'ha farro onore.
> (*Inf.* 1.85–87)

"But you are my master, my author," Dante cries, "the one source
of that style for which I am so honored." That said, Dante calls attention to the beasts that menace him, to which Virgil replies that he
must undertake another route if he wishes to escape this savage place.
As for the beasts, here some scholars find the basis for a political interpretation, since Virgil predicts that a greyhound will come, defeat
the beasts, and restore Italy.[12]

Virgil offers himself as guide and gives a preview of the journey
before them. He will take Dante down through a realm where he
will hear the howls of desperation of those who lament their "second
death." On they will travel to another realm, where there are souls
who can accept their pain because it is temporary and a prelude to
their joining the blessed. As for the blessed, Virgil tells Dante, he will
need another guide to go among them. At that point a soul more worthy than Virgil will become Dante's guide. "I'll leave you in her care
when I depart."

The schema of the *Commedia* is all here. To escape the dark wood,
Dante must descend into hell, the realm of despair, go on to purgatory,

where hope consoles the souls encountered there, and then on to the realm of the blessed, guided by an unnamed woman.

Why Virgil? There is a plethora of reasons for Dante's choice. The first is the one first given. Dante is a poet who learned from the master Virgil the pleasing style that has brought him fame. Who could better guide a poet than another poet? Moreover, when they visit Limbo, the first circle of hell and Virgil's permanent home, from which he has come to aid Dante, our author will be admitted into the company of the greatest poets as their peer. All this is presented as more or less matter of fact—another indication of Dante's estimate of his achievement as a poet. There is no false modesty here, sometimes none at all. Another reason is that in the sixth book of the *Aeneid*, Virgil had taken Aeneas into the underworld to see once more his late beloved father, Anchises. Scholars note the parallels and discrepancies between the underworld of the *Aeneid* and that into which we are about to descend. In any case, Virgil is a knowledgeable guide.

Yet what an odd choice to guide Dante to heaven—though only to it, not into it, as Virgil himself remarks. As a pagan, unredeemed by the grace of Christ, paradise is closed to him, and that means human happiness in its fullness cannot be his. Virgil will lead Dante to Limbo, which is his eternal place, and there they will meet other good pagans, Plato and Aristotle and poets such as Horace and Homer. Limbo is the place reserved for those who had only the light of natural reason to guide them through life. The Jews had revelation, of course, a covenant with God, and we will find half the celestial rose in the *Paradiso* allotted to them. The difference between the sons of Abraham and pagans is that the Israelites lived in the expectation of the Messiah. Thus, when Christ came the Jews could be saved by his sacrifice; they had anticipated the grace won by Christ.

Note that there are no alternative paths to ultimate happiness. There is but one path, the one on which we follow Christ and by participating in his grace can merit salvation. Nothing like the longing for the Messiah can be expected among the pagans. But if Limbo is where the highest natural happiness is enjoyed, the place does not seem joyful. Indeed, there is a melancholy air about it. This is due, as Virgil himself makes clear, to the fact that its inhabitants have become aware that, through no fault of their own, they have missed out on supernatural happiness.

We may think that there is something unjust about this. Why were the chosen people chosen and the pagans left to their own devices? Isn't it unfair of God not to admit pagans into heaven? This difficulty only makes sense if we think that paradise, that is, supernatural happiness, the sharing in God's very life and the sight of God even as we are seen by Him, is naturally owed to anyone. But paradise is wholly gratuitous. Things are owed us because of our nature, but supernatural happiness, as the adjective suggests, is not among them. A pagan in Limbo might lament that he was born where and when he was, but of course he has no assurance that, born later and elsewhere, he would have availed himself of the opportunity for salvation.

Limbo is the acknowledgment that many pagans lived good lives simply in the light of natural reason. There is less talk of Limbo in Catholic circles now, and Vatican II's Dogmatic Constitution on the Church, *Lumen Gentium*, seems to open up extraordinary ways in which non-Catholic Christians, Jews, Muslims, and even atheists might win through to paradise. If they live by their best lights, *Lumen Gentium* suggests, this can enable them to participate, even unbeknownst, in the grace of Christ. Whether or not this is a development of doctrine, the essential point remains true. There is no salvation except through the grace of Christ. Other medievals did not hesitate to canonize the good pagans; Peter Abelard was particularly prodigal in this regard, and Virgil appears in the stained glass windows of Chartres. But however the matter is approached, a great mystery still lurks here. Why are some given special opportunities and help, and others are not? The mystery of predestination accompanies us through Dante's pilgrim voyage and is one of the last topics dealt with in the poem.

In any case, one of Virgil's roles—or one aspect of his role—is to represent reason, that is, the natural order. Plato and Aristotle had lasting things to say about our overall aim in life and how it can be attained, given our nature. They lay out the virtue and character required of us if we are to do the right deed for the right reason in the fluctuating circumstances of life. But what relevance can Plato's *Politics* or Aristotle's *Nicomachean Ethics* have if we are called to an end undreamt of by the philosophers? "For Christ did not send me to baptize, but to preach the Good News, and not to preach that in terms of philosophy in which the crucifixion of Christ cannot be expressed" (1 Cor. 1:17).

In commenting on this passage, St. Thomas remarks that the happiness presented and discussed by Aristotle is no longer the ultimate end of human existence. Thomas, who was a great admirer of Aristotle and wrote commentaries on a dozen of his treatises, did not regard the philosophy of the ancients as having merely historical interest— that is, he did not think of it as merely what people used to think who had not heard the Good News. For him, the relationship between natural and supernatural happiness is very similar to the more general relationship between nature and "supernature," or divine grace. In the familiar phrase, grace builds on nature and does not destroy it. Grace presupposes nature.

If we ask ourselves what man's ultimate end is, we can mean either of two questions. First, what is meant by the phrase "ultimate end"? And second, given that meaning, what could serve as or play the role of ultimate end for us? If by our ultimate end we mean happiness— that which when obtained is sufficient, requires nothing else, is stable, and so forth—we can then go on to ask whether pleasure or power or wealth or fame and the like could fulfill the requirements of an ultimate end. Both Plato and Aristotle provide conclusive reasons why none of these can be the be-all and end-all of human life. Can anything?

Since rational activity is peculiar to man, Aristotle observed, man's fulfillment or happiness will lie in performing this function well. "Virtue" is the substantive name for this adverbial modification of our distinctive activity. A good physician is one who performs the work of the physician well; a good novelist is a writer who produces excellent novels; and so on. Once we know the function, we know that the virtue or perfect accomplishment of that function is what makes the one performing it good.

The fly in the ointment here is that "rational activity" seems to have a plurality of meanings, not just one. Thus, if the virtue or excellence of rational activity is the key to happiness, a plurality of virtues must be required for human happiness, unless perhaps we want to say that only one of the many meanings of "rational activity" counts.[13]

My point in recalling such debates is, first, to suggest another reason for the choice of Virgil as Dante's guide, and second, to underscore the layered approach that Dante takes to human life and its destiny. Only the union with God that is promised us as a reward for faith fulfills the notion of an ultimate end perfectly. What the ancient philosophers sketched as fulfilling the notion is true up to a point, but it is inadequate. It is true to the degree that it is a correct account of human nature and of what would fulfill it. It is inadequate because we see that such a virtuous life only imperfectly realizes the notion of the ultimate end. Thomas thought he had found in Aristotle the admission that his account of what constitutes our happiness does not meet all the requirements of an ultimate end. That is, the happiness we can naturally achieve is imperfect.

Like Thomas Aquinas, Dante views the natural as presupposed by the supernatural and as entering into the richer Christian vision of human destiny, as a constituent of it. The sometimes puzzling intermingling by Dante of pagan mythology and Christian doctrine underscores this view. Thomas sought to create a synthesis of all that could be known by natural reason together with the truths learned only by way of revelation. Dante undertakes a similar task in the *Commedia*.

Donna che si compiange: The Lady who weeps

Dante and Virgil, as we have seen, will travel first through the realm of despair, where dwell those who have died "a second death," having lost not only mortal but also (a happy) immortal life; and then on to a realm where they will find, despite the fire, souls content in the hope that they will eventually move on to the third realm, that of the blessed. In the realm of the blessed Dante will need another guide. Virgil adds (in a puzzling statement) that the ruler of that realm does not wish Virgil to enter it, "because I rebelled against his law" (*Inf.* 1.125).[14]

Now we have two guides, Virgil and the as yet unnamed woman who will take over after the first two realms. Why both? (As we shall see, there is yet a third guide in the last three cantos of the poem, and lesser guides and mentors along the way.) Virgil gives his answer in the second canto.

The canto begins with an invocation of the Muses, indicating, as does the presence of Virgil, Dante's blending of the classical and the Christian. The fact that Virgil told the story of the founding of Rome—the destiny of Aeneas chosen for him in the celestial empyrean, that is, in heaven—and the fact that the Roman empire was providentially the setting for Christianity, must explain Dante's choice of Virgil. That is, Virgil celebrated Rome, the city "u' siede il successor del maggior Piero": "where the successor of the great Peter sits" (*Inf.* 2.24), and to which Paul came as missionary.

The mention of Paul provides Dante with a way of expressing his fear at the prospect Virgil has put before him. "Io non Enëa, io non Paulo sono": "I'm no Aeneas, I'm not Paul" (*Inf.* 2.32). To allay that fear, Virgil tells why he has come to rescue Dante.

> Io era tra color che son sospesi,
> e donna mi chiamò beata e bella,
> tal che di comandare io la richiesi.
> Lucevan li occhi suoi più che la stella;
> e cominciommi a dir soave e piana,
> con angelica voce, in sua favella.
> (*Inf.* 2.52–57)

> I was among those who are suspended (in Limbo), where a lady
> came to me so blessed and beautiful that I begged to obey her
> command. Her eyes were brighter than the stars and she began to
> speak to me with a sweet angelic voice.

Virgil thus presents himself as a volunteer as well; how could he not wish to serve so fair and beautiful a woman who speaks in such angelic tones? She begins with equal courtesy, telling the Mantuan poet that his fame will endure as long as the world itself, and then gives Virgil his commission.

> L'amico mio, e non della ventura,
> nella diserta piaggia è impedito

sì nel cammin, che volt'è per paura;
  e temo che non sia già sì smarrito,
ch'io mi sia tardi al soccorso levata,
per quel ch'i' ho di lui nel cielo udito.
                              (*Inf.* 2.61–66)

My friend not by chance is hindered on his way on a deserted
hillside and because of fear has been turned away; I fear that he
has already become so lost that I may be too late to help him,
or so I have heard of him in heaven.

The speaker identifies herself as Beatrice, and we have no trouble
identifying who her friend is from the opening of the previous canto.
If it had not occurred to us before, we now see the nature of Dante's
perilous condition at the outset of the *Commedia*. The physical dan-
gers, the menacing beasts, point to a greater evil: that he has gone
so far astray that her help will come too late. All this she has heard
of him in heaven, she says, and then, in partial explanation of the
choice of Virgil, adds that poet can speak to poet persuasively. This
will console her, and she adds that only her love has led her to Limbo
from the place to which she longs to return. When she returns, she
promises Virgil to sing his praises to the Lord.

Is Beatrice, then, the principal cause of the journey that lies ahead,
the journey that has as its aim to rescue Dante from impending per-
dition and recall him to the right path? Beatrice tells Virgil that there
is another gentle lady who, although in heaven, weeps from distress
at Dante's condition. That gentle lady turned to St. Lucy and told her
that her "faithful one" had need of her, whereupon Lucy came to Beatrice and wondered why she had not gone to Dante's aid. This visit
from Lucy motivates Beatrice, of whom Lucy says that no one in the
world is more concerned for Dante's welfare. Now here she is, braving
hell itself, in order to enlist Virgil's help.

Thus, a hierarchy of three women stands behind the choice of
Virgil. Beatrice has been alerted—or reminded—by Lucy of the par-
lous condition into which the man who loves her has fallen. But Lucy,
too, has been prompted by another, who weeps because of the condition into which Dante and so many others have fallen:

Donna è gentil nel ciel che si compiange
di questo 'mpedimento . . .

(*Inf.* 2.94–95)

There is a gentle lady in heaven who weeps at this distress.

With this woman we come to the end of the chain. She, who is forever nameless in hell (as is Christ), is of course the Blessed Virgin Mary, introduced in terms of the compassion that she feels for poor sinners.

It is noteworthy that Mary is first introduced in the *Comedy* as the compassionate one, as she who weeps at our distress. *Celle qui pleure*—she who weeps—is the way Our Lady of La Salette is described. Mary is the Mother of Mercy who longs for all to share in the great happiness that has been won for them by her Son. It is also important to note that she is not our sole mediator. She is only the first among created mediators. There are also the saints, such as St. Lucy, and Beatrice, whose invocation on our behalf is so important in the economy of salvation. Mary describes Dante to Lucy as "your faithful one," indicating the devotion that Dante had to this martyr of Syracuse who had become the patron of those with eye trouble (one of Dante's afflictions). But the heavenly scene put before us makes clear that it is Mary, first and above all, who is moved by Dante's dangerous condition. The dark wood is clearly a metaphor for his sinful condition, and Mary, moved to pity by his state, speaks to Lucy, who in turn speaks to Beatrice. And Beatrice descends into hell and speaks to Virgil. Mary, however, is at the beginning of Dante's pilgrim journey and the principal explanation for it.

Mary's appearance may seem merely a cameo, a device to get the action started, but nothing could be further from the truth. Mary's distress is communicated to Lucy and Beatrice, and in each case a gentle chiding is involved. How could Lucy fail to notice the plight of her faithful one? Lucy in turn asks Beatrice, How she could forget the one who loved her so? Can she not hear his anguished cry as he wars against the death that menaces him? This death is above all that "second death" of those in hell. Lucy and Beatrice may have forgotten Dante, but Mary has not, and out of pity she calls the others into action.

For all that, Mary seems to drop out of the picture while Virgil and Dante descend through the circle of hell to the lake of ice at the center of the world, in which Lucifer is frozen. There is one other allusion to her intercession on the way down, but, again, she is never named in hell. That would be as unfitting as invoking the name of Christ in hell. This is the realm where all hope has been abandoned. If Dante is being led through it, it is because he needs this way to reach his final destination. He needs a vivid reminder of the state of souls after death and how their state is explained by the free acts they performed while alive. It is a dramatic and moral lesson, meant to lead him from the misery of sin to eternal happiness. And not just him, of course. This singular Florentine poet stands for all of us, and Mary's concern for him embraces each of us. Only after Dante and Virgil, having reached the frozen pit of hell and ascended through the opposite hemisphere, "emerge to see again the stars" (*Inf.* 34.139) does the role of Mary become central again, until, at the end of the *Commedia*, her intercession gains for Dante a glimpse of the glory that awaits in heaven.

THREE

The Seven Storey Mountain

Let us not think impiously
nor envy anyone
nor if struck in turn offend
but evil overcome with good.

Be absent from our hearts
wrath, envy and pride,
and away with avarice,
the root of every evil.
        —*Liturgia horarum (Liturgy of the Hours),*
        hebd 3, ad officium lectionis

Per una lagrimetta: Thanks to a little tear

In the second canto of the *Purgatorio*, the souls who disembark on
the island where the great mountain rises sing from Psalm 113(114),
"When Israel went out of Egypt," and we are of course reminded of
the way in which Dante used its verses in the letter to Can Grande
to illustrate the senses of Scripture. The anagogical meaning was the
soul's escape from this mortal world to paradise, and that is what we

see these souls engaged upon. First they must be purged of the stain of the sins they committed, even though they have been forgiven already. In fact, delay is a note struck early in the cantica, but not so as to blur the great difference between this realm and the preceding one. Hell is the realm of despair; Purgatory is the realm of hope. The souls here are assured of their salvation and their eventual entry into glory, and they are quite willing to suffer the delays that purgation entails.

Souls are brought by boat from Ostia, etymologically located at the mouth of the Tiber, where usually they find it difficult to book passage and have to wait. At the moment, however, things have been speeded up. This is due no doubt to the Jubilee Year, during which the pope extended certain favors to the dead.

The continuing role of Dante's *tre donne*, his three ladies, becomes apparent. When Virgil, confronting a forbidding Cato, guardian of Purgatory, explains their coming up from hell, he invokes Beatrice, the lady who came from heaven to enlist him as a guide for Dante. Cato is thereby placated. After the first night on the island, Dante finds that he has been transported by Lucy up to the Gate of Peter, where Purgatory proper begins. And Mary? Her role is the most important one, and we can watch it expand as we proceed.

There are two initial levels on the lower slopes of the island, called ante-Purgatory, where souls must wait before they can begin their purgation: the level of the excommunicated and the level of the late repentant (of which there are three kinds, the indolent, the unshriven, and the preoccupied). Among the unshriven is Buonconte, who was killed in the battle of Campaldino, a battle in which Dante himself had fought. But how can an unshriven soul end in purgatory, with the assurance of heaven to sustain his hope? Buonconte describes his final moment on earth for Dante:

> Quivi perdei la vista e la parola;
> nel nome di Maria finì, e quivi
> caddi, e rimasa la mia carne sola.
>   Io dirò vero, e tu 'l ridì tra ' vivi:
> l'angel di Dio mi prese, e quel d'inferno
> gridava: "O tu del ciel, perché mi privi?

Tu te ne porti de costui l'etterno
per una lagrimetta che 'l mi toglie.
(*Purg.* 5.100–107)

There I lost sight and speech just as I uttered Mary's name, then
fell, and only my flesh remained. I tell you truly and you tell it to
the living, the angel of God came for me and the angel of hell
complained, "O you of heaven, why do you deprive me? For just
one little tear you carry off his eternal part."

Buonconte, though unshriven, died repentant with the name of
Mary on his lips. Tell my story, he urges Dante, and describe the rage
of the devil who came to claim me only to find that an angel had
snatched away his prey. O thief of heaven! The angel came in effect as
the messenger of Mary. We are made aware of the power and effica-
ciousness of the Mother of God. And this raises a problem. Does her
intervention make a mockery of the basic premise of the *Comedy*?

The allegorical meaning of the great poem is the way in which
human beings, by their free acts, justly merit punishment or reward.
But Buonconte's single tear *in ictu mortis,* the murmuring of Mary's
name, sweeps away a lifetime of freely chosen and awful deeds as if
they had never been. Deathbed conversions seem to make the way
one has lived inconsequential.

A first response to this would be to notice that Buonconte's case
is that of most of us, not a rare exception. *Sero te amavi,* Augustine
laments: Late have I loved thee. Every conversion must seem to
come late and after deeds we would rather not remember. Of course,
those deeds leave their mark on the soul. Buonconte must mount all
seven levels of the mountain of Purgatory proper before his soul is
fit to see God. The words *Ave, Maria* will be heard increasingly as
the poem continues, and we may remember the second half of that
prayer as it developed: "Holy Mary, Mother of God, pray for us sinners, now and at the hour of our death."[1] It thus becomes a prayer for
a happy death. And who could not take comfort from Buonconte's
near escape from the realm of despair?

Furthermore, late or even deathbed conversions do not negate
the assumptions of the poem. Every moral decision takes place in

an instant, we might say, however prolonged the reflection leading up to it. The moment of choice is a moment, after all. And in the last moments of life one is still capable of making a choice that defines the state of one's soul. Repentance makes the one who was estranged from God by sin into God's friend again. All that is true, but it in turn may seem to trivialize Buonconte's story. He himself is awed by what happened, which is one reason he wants his story told. The other is because his story can be a consolation to the living.

Beatrice may be the "open sesame" with Cato, Lucy may transport Dante in a dream to Peter's Gate, but by Mary's intercession, souls are saved. I don't suggest that this is an exact division of labor. After all, Lucy is a saint, and Dante has clearly canonized Beatrice—just as in the Circle of the Sun in the *Paradiso* he anticipates the canonizations of Thomas Aquinas and Bonaventure. The last two are not the most surprising additions to the calendar of the saints in that circle, and the intercession of the saints is efficacious, but, as elsewhere in the poem, these lesser intercessors are instruments of the Mother of Mercy. When Virgil tells Dante of the limitations of the human intellect in understanding the divine plan, he explains that if this were not so, if all were clear to us now, "mestier non era parturir Maria"—it would not have been necessary for Mary to give birth (*Purg.* 3.39). This apparent aside draws our attention to the unique role Mary plays in our salvation. She bore the Incarnate God by whose stripes we are healed. Without the mother there would be no son, and without the son, no salvation. No other mere creature plays so essential a role in the great drama of salvation as Mary.

Philosophical Prelude to the Purgatorio

It is helpful to pause here and reflect further on the logic that underlies the *Purgatorio*, guided, as was Dante, by Thomas Aquinas. Our appetites, as the word suggests, seek something. They pull us toward their objects as the end they desire, and therefore they pull us toward goods. The *good* is that which all things seek. This is indeed a comprehensive statement. Appetite and desire are not confined to human agents. "Water seeks its own level" would not have been a metaphor for Dante. The whole of creation and every creature in it is an expression of the goodness that is God. Creatures, we might say, have goodness in various degrees, but God *is* goodness. The whole of creation tends toward him as its ultimate end.

Any action aims at some good, and a created good will always be a particular good, not, needless to say, the sum total of goodness. Water slakes thirst, bread hunger. The sense appetites thus bear on particular goods—food, drink, the pleasure associated with the performance of natural functions. In his disquisition on love in *Purgatorio* 17, Virgil distinguishes importantly between natural and rational love: *o naturale o d'animo* (*Purg.* 17.93).

"Fish gotta swim, birds gotta fly"—these exemplify what is meant by natural love or desire, but "I gotta love one man till I die" does not. We do not decide to want our hunger and thirst slaked; men do not *decide* to be attracted to women, or women to men; it is not a decision to seek pleasure and avoid pain. Such natural desires are the infrastructure of human action. They become *d'animo* when a person decides how, when, and what will slake her thirst, and of course how much and how this will fit into her overall good. We get no credit or blame for natural love or desire; but as moral agents we become responsible, that is, answerable for our choices. A natural attraction is consciously pursued. A man or woman does not marry just any person who catches the wandering eye.

Humans are layered beings, and they are not the first creatures in the cosmos. (Those are the angels.) The great universal for Dante is love. It permeates the universe because it is at its origin. Creation is the product of the divine love, and all creatures have some share in the fullness of goodness that is God. God is the love that moves the sun and other stars, and all the sublunary world as well. Creatures embody a hierarchy of loves, from the fall of the stone, to water seeking its own level, to the more complicated seeking involved in the growth and nourishing of plants. The move from the inanimate to the animate world (which is not coterminous with what Virgil calls *d'animo*) is the move to the moral order. The simplest of material beings have a single good that they seek; they are, in St. Thomas's phrase, determined to one object as their good. For living things, "seeking good" becomes more complicated: a plant, for example, grows up and down and reaches out in every direction, enabling it to grow and flourish. (That is the natural habitat of the word "flourishing"—flowering.) Seeking good is more indeterminate with plants than with rocks and water. But already it is layered. Plants, like rocks, can also be weighed, and they fall when dropped. The "desires" that plants share with lesser things are not peculiar to them, but they are there.

If the higher, vegetative level includes lower, less complicated loves as well as what is distinctive of it, the lower level can be called natural—and is—by contrast with the desires of living things. But the distinctive activity of plants is natural, too, in the sense that it is not chosen. The two levels in plants are also present in the next level, that of animals. Like plants, they grow and take nourishment, but beasts have an awareness that we would not attribute to plants (except, of course, in fiction, as in the Roald Dahl story in which a man hears the screaming of the grass as it is being mowed). Pursuit of the pleasurable and avoidance of harm manifests itself in increasingly complicated ways as we move up the created hierarchy. When we come to man, we are invited to see him as a microcosmos. We share desires with lower realms of being, but we are beings whose distinctive love is prompted by knowledge more comprehensive than that which guides other animals' actions.

We are aware of the freedom we have in our pursuit of the goods we do not choose to want, goods such as food and drink. Call these goods natural, and we grasp what Virgil means by *d'animo*. For the human agent, the particular ends of natural desires are brought under a comprehensive desire for the good—for goodness itself—and they will be compared and then chosen in the light of their relation to our overall good. The young man knocking at the brothel door is looking for God. This initially startling remark by the novelist Bruce Marshall nicely summarizes the human case.

Our choices bear on particular objects as we relate them to goodness as such. The human pursuit of food or drink or sex—objects our appetites do not choose to want—is the *conscious* pursuit of those particular goods, and the human task is to relate the love of such things to our comprehensive good. However mistaken we may be in judging that relation, our actions are always a pursuit of things under the aegis of goodness. Particular goods are to be sought in relation to goodness as such. The pathetic boy at the brothel door mistakenly sees what he wants as related to that comprehensive good.

Even when we correctly seek a particular good in relation to the comprehensive good, we become aware that it cannot completely assuage our desire. Augustine wrote in his *Confessions*, "You have made us for yourself, O God, and our hearts are restless until they rest in thee." Our awareness of ourselves and of the arena in which we act lifts us above the irrational animals. Each of us is a microcosm, the epitomization of the cosmos, whose distinctive capacities—intellect and will—enable us consciously and freely to direct our lives. The great message of the *Comedy* is that our free will makes us responsible for ordering our deeds to the true good. We can succeed or fail. But whether in success or failure, what draws us on is the good.

The Logic of Purgatory, Continued

Only after passing through ante-Purgatory (the location of the excommunicated and late repentant) and then ascending the first three levels of the mountain proper, where souls are purged of the effects of pride, envy, and anger, does Virgil explain to Dante the rationale of this graded purgation.

> "Né creator né creatura mai,"
> cominciò el, "figliuol, fu sanza amore,
> o naturale o d'animo; et tu 'l sai.
>   Lo naturale è sempre sanza errore,
> Ma l'altro puote errar per malo obietto
> o per troppo o per poco di vigore.
>   Mentre ch'elli è nel primo ben diretto,
> e ne' secondi sé stesso misura,
> esser non può cagion di mal diletto;
>   ma quando al mal si torce, o con più cura
> o con men che non dee corre nel bene,
> contra 'l fattore adovra sua fattura.
>
> (*Purg.* 17.91–102)

Son, he began, neither creator nor creature ever was without love, either natural or of the soul, as you know. The natural is always without error, but the other can err because of a bad object, or because of too much or too little vigor. As long as the first is well directed and tends to secondary goods within measure, it cannot be cause of evil delight, but when it turns to evil or seeks the good with too much or too little care, the creature acts against its Creator.

Fault can arise, then, either from pursuing evil or by excessive or defective pursuit of the good. Virgil underscores the fact that love is the source of all action, not only virtuous action. But if this is true, and if love is of the good, how can there be bad action? The answer involves the fact that evil is always parasitic on the good.

Among the things we are not free to love are, first, God, goodness itself; everything is loved *sub ratione boni.* Nor can we fail to love ourselves. So what is left, to explain love twisted toward evil?

> Resta, se dividendo bene stimo,
> che 'l mal che s'ama è del prossimo; ed esso
> amor nasce in tre modi in vostro limo.
> (*Purg.* 17.112–114)

There remains, if I have distinguished well, the evil one wishes for his neighbor, and this your clay gives birth to in three ways.

It is in relation to our neighbor that a threefold fault can enter in. Here we are given the explanation of the first three levels proper of Purgatory and the capital sins that define them. Sometimes we want to excel and thereby wish our neighbor to be abased. Sometimes we fear to lose honor or fame by our neighbor's ascendancy, and thus we wish him or her to fail. And sometimes this leads us to take vengeance against others whose good fortune threatens to excel our own. In short, we can be guilty of pride, envy, or anger. The perverted love involved in such sinful behavior is purged *di sotto*, below, that is, on the first three levels of the mountain. Moreover, if we respond with lukewarm love to the good we recognize, we are guilty of another sin, sloth or *acedia.* This sin defines the fourth level, which serves as a kind of divider of the mountain. Below it are sins that involve wishing our neighbor harm; sloth itself is defective love of the good; and the three upper levels are concerned with the effects of sins arising from disordered love of the good. These are covetousness, gluttony, and lust. Thus Dante has defined the capital sins in terms of the great wellspring of action, love of the good.

> Ciascun confusamente un bene apprende
> nel qual si queti l'animo, e desira;
> per che di giugner lui ciascun contende.
>
> (*Purg.* 17.127–129)

> Each one of us confusedly grasps the good in which the soul can rest and desires it: thus all seek to reach that good.

Lo naturale è sempre sanza errore: The natural is never wrong

We are given this map of the second kingdom, or, more precisely, a description and comparison of the seven levels or terraces of the mountain, when Dante and Virgil are moving from the third to the fourth terrace. And these terraces are divided into three groups. To repeat, the first group comprises the first three terraces; the second is a class with one member, the fourth terrace; and the third comprises the remaining three terraces. Reversing the ordering of the *Inferno*, where Dante descended into more and more serious sins and their punishments, the *Purgatorio* commences with the most serious of the capital sins. Souls then ascend to the least serious sins. One sign of this ordering is that Dante finds the ascent less fatiguing as he travels higher on the mountain. What is the basis for the three groupings?

The fundamental principle, as we have seen, is that every human act is prompted by love of the good, and defective or sinful acts are those involving a defective love of the good.

> Quinci comprender puoi ch'esser convene
> amor sementa in voi d'ogne virtute
> e d'ogne operazion che merta pene.
>
> (*Purg.* 17.103–105)

> Thus you understand that love is the seed in you of every virtue
> as well as of every act deserving of punishment.

Performing our distinctive act well is what is meant by virtue, and performing it badly is vice.[2] Our distinctive act is freely and consciously to direct ourselves to the comprehensive good by means of the particular goods we choose.

Does Dante think that we begin with a clear and developed notion of the comprehensive good that draws us on? Hardly. He is an Aristotelian who knows that human knowledge begins in generalities, in a confused grasp, and only gradually attains clarity. Similarly, Boethius in his colloquy with Dame Philosophy is told of this implicit desire for happiness: "'Whither?' I asked. 'To true happiness,' she answered, 'of which your mind also dreams but cannot see it for what it is because you are occupied with images.'"[3] Aristotle's *Nicomachean Ethics* finds in our natural and irrepressible desire for happiness our ultimate end. But it remains to determine what precisely that happiness is. Our pursuit of happiness does not await that clarification, of course; rather, the clarification is demanded by the given universal human desire for happiness, whatever it might be.

To the Manichean, some things are evil in themselves and others are good in themselves, and moral good and evil simply await our choices. Dante will have none of this. Our choices are always of something good. It is when we choose a good in a disordered way, that is, not relating it to the good for which we are made, that our acts are evil. Our sense appetites simply draw us to goods—food, drink, and sex are goods—but because of reason and will, we are not the toys of our sense appetites. "If sex were all then every trembling hand could make us squeak, like dolls, the wished for words," wrote Wallace Stevens.[4] We are drawn to but not compelled by sensible goods. Virgil explains the layout of Purgatory that we have been paraphrasing against this background.

The movement of will toward our grasp of the good is natural, not free. Nor do we need instruction in order to seek our own good. Nor, says Virgil, can we as creatures think ourselves sufficient unto ourselves, divorced from God. We cannot hate the source of the fact that we exist and are what we are. In that sense, love of God is natural to us. So again, how do we go wrong? If we cannot hate ourselves or God, we can still wish harm to our neighbor. When we see our neighbor's greatness as a threat to and detraction from our own, and want to suppress him, we are guilty of pride. My excellence, my flourishing, and my good are taken to be diminished by the excellence, flourishing, and good of my neighbor as subtracting from my own. In a disordered pursuit of my own good, I wish harm to my neighbor and want him brought low so that my height might thereby be increased. Pride is the source of all other moral evils. That is why it comes first and is expiated on the first terrace of Purgatory.

> è chi podere, grazia, onore e fama
> teme di perder perch' altri sormonti,
> onde s'attrista sì che 'l contrario ama;
>   (*Purg.* 17.118–120)

And there is he who fears to lose favor, honor and fame because another surpasses him, grieves and loves the contrary.

Envy arises out of pride. We are saddened when others rise above us in excellence, fearing that we are thereby losing our own "fame, favor and honor." The envious brood over and are made gloomy by the success of others.

> ed è chi per ingiuria par ch'aonti,
> sì che si fa de la vendetta ghiotto,
> e tal convien che 'l male altrui impronti.
>   (*Purg.* 17.121–123)

And there is he who feels himself so degraded by insult that he becomes greedy for vengeance; such a one must crave another's harm.

Thus, in the logic of vice, pride begets envy and envy begets wrath. And so, being purged of pride, souls find the next purgation easier, and the next easier still.

This disquisition of Virgil, remember, takes place after he has accompanied Dante up the first three levels of Purgatory, which involve *triforme amor*, three forms of disordered love. Thus far, it is a retrospective. In the next canto Dante begs Virgil to continue. What is this love by which you explain both virtue and vice?

Anna Maria Chiavacci Leonardi, in her introduction to and notes on canto 18 of the *Purgatorio*, stresses the peculiar personal importance of the continuing discussion for Dante. His poetic mentors, and indeed Dante as well, have described love as a fatality, as something that comes and simply overwhelms the person. The phrase "falling in love" retains something of this conception. But if love conquers all, in Ovid's famous phrase, how can we be free? Dante is about to reject the theory of love that had animated so much of his earlier poetry. If we are helpless before the assault of love—this was Francesca's attempted self-exculpation in the *Inferno*—how can we be praised or blamed? In reply, Virgil explains the logic further.

The first movement of the will toward an object, like that of intellect, is natural and thus not free. The mind grasps an object, and the will desires the good. But to choose this good or that is not determined. In that respect we are free, and it is in the pursuit of particular goods that we fare well or ill morally. We are not determined to a disordered pursuit of goods, that is, a pursuit that does not relate particular goods to the ultimate good. Nor is it necessary that we pursue them in an ordered way. To choose is our essential moral task.

Of course, there is something in the notion that we fall in love and that there are fatal, or better fateful, attractions of one person to another. Wasn't it Pascal who said that all that was needed to alter the course of history was to add an inch to Cleopatra's nose? Accidents of feature and gesture first attract us, and the pulse quickens. Are we helpless, then? Was it kismet that we met and kissed? Lovers love to think so. Nor is it fanciful to think that our beloved was meant for us, and vice versa. But there must be acquiescence or rejection of this passionate response. We are, with whatever difficulty, free to pursue or not to pursue. Lovers at the altar give free consent to the attractions that brought them there. Despite all the lyrics of a thousand ballads, we are not slaves of love. Human love is a free act and may be virtuous or not.

Dante will return to the topics of love and free will in the *Paradiso*, when the question of predestination arises. But Virgil's explanation here will be sufficient for us to mount the terraces of Purgatory with Dante and eventually to see how the Blessed Virgin is the examplar of the virtues opposed to the capital sins.

Io dico d'Aristotele e di Plato: I speak of Plato and Aristotle

The role of Virgil and the fact that Cato, another pagan Roman, is the guardian of Purgatory bring back another matter that becomes clarified in this second cantica of the great poem.

Earlier, in speaking of a natural happiness, namely, an imperfect realization of the ultimate end of which men are capable, we saw that the ethical considerations that surround this topic are subsumed by the supernatural. People do not cease being human when they believe in the divine; their belief rides on and is affected by their natural activities—and vice versa, of course. Beatrice came to Limbo to enlist the help of Virgil, and when Virgil guides Dante to the first level of the *Inferno*, he meets the great poets and sages of antiquity. Its occupants are good in the way humans can become good by their own efforts, by possessing the natural virtues. In canto 3 of the *Purgatorio*, Virgil alludes to his companions in Limbo as great souls who thirsted in vain:

> e disïar vedeste sanza frutto
> tai che sarebbe lor disio quetato,
> ch'etternalmente è dato lor per lutto:
>   io dico d'Aristotile e di Plato
> e di molt'altri . . .
> (Purg. 3.40–44)

You saw the fruitless desire of those who would have their desire fulfilled but whose desire eternally laments; I speak of Aristotle and Plato and of many others.

What the pagan philosophers could not know of during their lifetimes, now, in eternity, is a source of pain. What might have been, but alas was nor for them. Having mentioned them, and there are many like them, Virgil bows his head *e rimase turbato*, troubled. The reader too is troubled.

That the good pagans are without fault is explicitly stated in his own case by Virgil in canto 7. Speaking to Sordello, he remarks, "I am Virgil, who failed to get to heaven only because I did not have the faith" (*Purg.* 7.7–8). But although Limbo is not a punishment for personal fault, it is an acknowledgment of the great divide between those who have accepted the grace of Christ and those who have not. The case of those who lived before they could have made the choice is particularly poignant. As discussed in chapter 1, because the good pagans in the afterlife become aware of their eternal separation from the supernatural order, from the vision of God that is the reward of believers, they could hardly be presented as joyful.

This points to the enormous difference between, on the one hand, morality or ethics—philosophical or natural accounts of how life should be led—and, on the other hand, Christian revelation. The *Inferno*, it is often pointed out, seems structured on the *Nicomachean Ethics* of Aristotle. Indeed, Virgil himself makes this clear in canto 11 of the *Inferno* when he explains the layout of the lower world to Dante. As they descend into ever more heinous sins, the levels are incontinence, violence, and malice. At the first level they encounter the lustful sinners, indelibly represented by Paolo and Francesca. These two are perhaps the most commented on characters in the great poem, and we may be puzzled by their attractiveness. Illicit, adulterous lovers, caught in the act, they were dispatched before they could repent and must drift through eternity in an endless embrace. As Francesca recounts, the reading of the tale of Lancelot and Guinevere first stirred their imaginations and then their desire. (What we read affects our actions.) An eternal embrace might not seem much of a hell for lovers, but what they sought in one another cannot be found there. Their wills were made for God, goodness itself, who alone can assuage their desire.

We are likely to imagine that this example of Dante's is a little harsh. We tend to think in these days that sins of the flesh are scarcely worth calling sins. Dante would allow only that other mortal sins are worse. The lower the depth of hell, the worse the sin, and the worse the sin, the more gradations of it Dante brings to our attention.

If the hierarchy of sins is based on Aristotle, on philosophical ethics, then the arrangement of Purgatory brings home to us the essential difference between Christianity and natural morality. At the outset of the *Purgatorio*, Cato is described as reflecting the light of four stars. Scholars tell us that these represent the four cardinal virtues: temperance, fortitude, justice, and prudence. Later those stars will fade and three others take their place, representing the theological virtues: faith, hope, and charity. If Aristotle's *Ethics* may be taken as a reliable indication of what unaided human reason can discover about how we should live our lives, where should one go for a sketch of Christian morality? The answer is, of course, to the Sermon on the Mount in Matthew 5–7.

Jesus begins his sermon with the beatitudes. One cannot think of a more dramatic way of showing that the New Law is not the Old Law, nor is it simply a repetition of the teaching of philosophers. The beatitudes fly in the face of our natural assumptions about human life.

There have been philosophers who reject Christ's claim to be the Son of God, yet want to retain the "ethics of Jesus" as defensible within the limits of reason alone. Their suggestion is that the Sermon on the Mount contains only what we would naturally recognize as reasonable guidance. This seems nonsense. As a practical matter, many find belief in the Incarnation much easier than acceptance of the advice that they should love their enemy, for example. Far from being a distillation of natural moral wisdom, the Sermon on the Mount seems to stand natural wisdom on its head.

> Blessed are the poor in spirit, for theirs is the kingdom of heaven.
> Blessed are the meek, for they shall possess the earth.
> Blessed are they who mourn, for they shall be comforted.
> Blessed are they who hunger and thirst after justice, for they shall be satisfied.
> Blessed are the merciful, for they shall obtain mercy.
> Blessed are the clean of heart, for they shall see God.
> Blessed are the peacemakers, for they shall be called children of God.
> Blessed are they who suffer persecution for justice's sake, for theirs is the kingdom of heaven. (Matt. 5:3–10)

Centuries of Christianity have made this list familiar, and some phi-losophers, forgetful of the context in which the beatitudes were given us, mistakenly have thought that this sermon is just what any good philosopher could say. I challenge them to name one, I mean, one speaking purely as a philosopher. To assert that our happiness is to be found in poverty of spirit, in meekness, in mourning, and in suf-fering persecution is scarcely to state the self-evident. It goes against the grain of our natural being. Not only would we not have natu-rally hit upon these guidelines for conduct, but we cannot possibly incorporate them into our lives by our own power. For this, grace is necessary—the abundance of God's generosity, the gratuitousness (to be redundant) of this elevation of sinful man to an end undreamt of by philosophers and incommensurate with our human nature. *O felix culpa*, St. Augustine said of original sin: Oh happy fault, meaning that the remedy for the Fall was an elevation to a condition higher than that lost by Adam's sin. Everyone in Purgatory knows that he or she got there by the grace of God and in no other way. And Mary is the mother of grace. No wonder the souls there chant "*Salve, Regina*" (*Purg.* 7.82).

St. Thomas on the Beatitudes

Like many other doctors of the Church, Thomas Aquinas commented on the chapters of Matthew that have come to be known as the Ser-mon on the Mount. Calling it a sermon may suggest that Jesus was preaching to a large crowd, but in Matthew, according to Thomas, that was not the case. He went up onto the mountain and, when he had sat down, his disciples joined him and "opening his mouth, he taught them." Thomas ponders the fact that Jesus sat. When he preached, he stood; this is a more intimate scene, and the sitting suggests the Lord's humility, already embodied in the fact that He is God become man. By thus lowering himself, he becomes more accessible to us, as he cannot be in the majesty of his divinity. Jesus's being seated reminds Thomas of the master before his class, where being seated is a matter of professorial dignity: "Quiet is needed for the study of wisdom."[5] Jesus's disciples came to him not only in body but in soul. "Opening his mouth" suggests to Thomas that Jesus had been silent for a long time. With Augustine, he sees this as indicating that the sermon will be both deep and long.

A problem arises for the exegete in the fact that these chapters in Matthew have a parallel in Luke (6:20ff.), and the two passages seem to differ, not least in the fact that in Luke, Jesus is clearly speaking to a great crowd of people; and Luke's account is much shorter than in Matthew, only part of a chapter. Thomas recalls the two solutions proposed by Augustine. The first is that these passages tell of two different occasions; Jesus first taught his disciples and then, after coming down from the mountain, found a crowd waiting and recapitulated the sermon for them. The second solution is that the mountain in question had "a level stretch" lower down, and it was to this that Jesus descended and found the crowd. Thomas prefers this second solution. When Jesus withdrew and his disciples joined him, he selected the twelve apostles from them, as Luke recounts, taught them first, then went down to teach the crowd. This accords with the end of the account in Matthew. "And it came to pass when Jesus had finished these words, that the crowds were astonished at his teaching" (Matt. 7:28–29).

A commentary that dwells in such detail on the opening verse promises to be, and is, a lengthy one. Moreover, it is typical of the biblical exegesis with which Dante would have been familiar: close reading of the text, reference to other scriptural passages that throw light on it, and the invocation of earlier commentaries, with particular reference to the fathers of the early Church.

Augustine wrote that the whole perfection of our life is contained in the beatitudes; thus Jesus stresses the end to which the teaching leads. That end is happiness, and, as Thomas notes, "happiness (beatitude) is what man chiefly desires."[6] So the Lord does three things here: he sets forth the prize to be won; formulates the precepts that direct us to it; and finally tells us how we can come to observe these precepts.

But people are not of one mind as to what happiness is, however true it is that they all desire it. Thomas lists four different understandings of the term. Some seek happiness in external goods; others seek happiness as the satisfaction of their will, in power; others seek happiness in the practice of the virtues of the active life; and finally others, like Aristotle, seek happiness in the contemplation of the divine. So which is the right view? They are all false, Thomas says, although not in the same way. Nonetheless, the Lord rejects them all.[7]

These four candidates for the meaning of human happiness are familiar ones, and we would expect Thomas to commend the fourth, namely, contemplation of the divine. This expectation is bolstered by his attributing it to Aristotle. That fourth view is as satisfying an account as we can expect from the philosopher—and Thomas tells us that Jesus rejects it (*reprobat*). The rejection is to be found in the beatitudes themselves.

The first conception of happiness, that it lies in external goods, is countered by "Blessed are the poor in spirit." The second, the imposition of one's will on others, is countered by "Blessed are the merciful." And because men have several appetites, each must be addressed. The irascible appetite leads to the desire for vengeance, and this is countered by "Blessed are the meek." The concupiscible appetite aims at joy and pleasure, and this is countered by "Blessed are they who mourn." Finally, there is the will, which is twofold in that it seeks two things: first, that it be constrained by no higher law; second, that it may make subjects of others. That is, the will wants to excel and subdue, and the Lord teaches the opposite. "Blessed are they who hunger and thirst after justice" is the rejection of the first, and "Blessed are the merciful" again is the rejection of the second.

The third conception of happiness placed it in the practice of the virtues of the active life; this is a mistake, Thomas claims, but less so than the preceding accounts, because the active life is the *via ad beatitudinem*. And that is why the Lord does not reject it as evil but stresses that it is a *way* to happiness. How so? Such a virtue as temperance has for its end the agent, the "cleansing of the heart," since it enables him or her to conquer passions. Other virtues are aimed at other people, and their end is peace: *opus iustitiae est pax*. That is the point of "Blessed are the clean of heart, for they shall see God" and "Blessed are the peacemakers."

As for the view that happiness consists in contemplation of the divine, Thomas holds that the Lord rejects it as an end that we could achieve in our earthly, temporal lives, but otherwise it is true;

happiness does consist in contemplation of the most intelligible object, namely, God—"for they shall see God." That is the end to which all precepts point; that is the end to which we are called, and this makes the fourth account of happiness inadequate. But that account is as far as philosophy can take us. Moral virtues such as temperance and justice have a higher telos than any mere philosopher could imagine. And this has the consequence, since such happiness is above our nature, that the acquired virtues, those of which Aristotle speaks, must be complemented by what Thomas calls the infused virtues (virtues given us by divine grace) as well as by the three theological virtues.

Thomas underscores the novelty of this teaching by contrasting it with the Old Law, which promised happiness on this earth, in joy and song, whereas the New Law speaks of mourning as blessed. And the chief object of mourning is the death of loved ones. The mourner receives no consolation for his loss, and the Lord asks that we live our lives in mourning. If we mourn bodily death, all the more should we mourn spiritual death; it is for sin that we should mourn, and this entails making satisfaction for having committed it. The follower of Christ turns away from the pleasures recommended by the world. This Christian mourning receives consolation: spiritual and eternal goods and the love of God, rather than temporal and passing ones.

Thomas discusses the Sermon on the Mount in great detail, but this brief paraphrase gives the flavor of his exegesis and shows how Jesus's teaching surpasses and goes against mere philosophical teaching. It is the plain rejection of the first two views of our happiness, which locate it in pleasure and power. The third and fourth views, inadequate in themselves, are also to that degree false—the practice of the virtues of the active life and such contemplation of the divine as the philosopher attains can never fulfill our heart's desire. But the practice of the moral virtues is a condition for the pursuit of happiness in the sense of contemplation, and the contemplation of the philosopher is an imperfect realization of the notion of ultimate end. It is contrasted, as we have seen, with the perfect realization, and that is to see God as He is, to be joined to Him in love. It was no defect in a philosopher such as Aristotle that he did not locate happiness in the beatific vision. Nothing he could know about human nature would suggest such an incommensurable object of our desires. The Christian believer is able to see the inadequacy of contemplation in the philosophical sense, not as a philosophical inadequacy but rather as falling short of what Jesus promises: "they shall see God." This does not render philosophical discussions pointless; far from it. But Dante, like St. Thomas, will always relate natural truths to the supernatural; only then can they be of real interest to the Christian. For the believer, the full and adequate account of human happiness is contained in the beatitudes. Anything less is—less; and the more is a matter of grace.

St. Thomas on the Capital Sins

The seven levels of Mount Purgatory represent the seven capital sins, from the effects of which souls must be purged before they are ready to enter paradise. For each of the capital sins there is an opposite virtue, and as we ascend the mountain we find that some event in the life of the Blessed Virgin is recalled in order to illustrate each of those virtues. But first, Thomas's account of the capital sins deserves mention.

For Thomas, to seek an end is to avoid its opposite, as the desire for food is the avoidance of or flight from hunger. All the capital sins involve a rationale for pursuit and avoidance, and the capital sins are distinguished insofar as there are distinctively different pursuits and avoidance. The good is what, by definition, attracts; thus, if the will avoids a good, this must be because of the way that good is regarded. After these prefatory remarks, in his *Disputed Questions on Evil* (*De malo*), Thomas does what we have learned to expect from him. There is a long tradition of Christian discussion of the capital sins, and he is aware of it. He is particularly indebted to the account of Gregory the Great. But Thomas further gives us what might almost be called a deduction of the capital sins.[8]

Thomas begins by discussing the term "capital" as it is used here. There are capital offenses, of course, but capital sins are so called because they are the source of other subsidiary sins. According to Thomas, there are four ways in which a sin can give rise to other sins, and he settles on the last for his definition:

There is a fourth way in which one sin can cause another, because of its end, insofar as a man commits one sin for the sake of the end of another sin, as avarice causes fraud. In this way one sin is caused by another actually and formally; and it is because of this mode of origin that they are called capital vices. (*De malo*, q. 8, a. 1, c)

That a sin can be ordered to the end of another sin can arise on the side of the sinner, who may be more prone to the one end than the other. More than this is meant by a capital sin, however. When the end of one sin is related to the end of another in such a way that, by and large, the one leads to the other, the first is the capital sin. Thus, the aim of fraud is deception, but fraud is aimed at monetary gain, the end of avarice. That is why avarice is called a capital vice or sin.

This requires that capital sins have ends desirable in themselves, to which the ends of the other vices can be ordered. Notice, Thomas goes on, that one pursues a good and flees the opposed evil, as the glutton seeks pleasure in food and flees the distress caused by the absence of food. So it is with the other vices. Capital sins can be fittingly distinguished according to the difference of good and evil, such that wherever there is a special reason for pursuit or avoidance, there we will find a distinct capital sin. By "good" we mean that which attracts appetite, so that if appetite avoids some good, it is because of some aspect of this good.

Man has a threefold good, namely, the good of the soul, the good of the body, and the good of external things. Pride or Vainglory is ordered to the good of the soul, which is a good of which we form an image, namely, the excellence of honor and glory. As for the good of the body pertaining to the preservation of the individual, food, Gluttony is ordered to it. The corporeal good that pertains to the conservation of the species as this involves the venereal is the concern of Lust. Avarice pertains to external goods. (*De malo*, q. 8, a. 1, c)

That gives us four capital sins. There are three more:

One retreats from the good insofar as it is an impediment to some good inordinately desired, and to such an impeding good, appetite moves in two ways, either by fleeing it or by rising in rebellion against it. Two capital sins arise from fleeing the good, depending on whether the impeding good is considered in itself or in another; in itself, as when a spiritual good impedes bodily rest or pleasure, and this is Acedia; in another, when the god of another impedes one's own excellence, and this is Envy, which is sadness at another's good; Wrath is the rising up against the good. (Ibid.)

The capital sins are distributed by Dante on the terraces of the *Purgatorio* in this ascending order: pride, envy, anger, sloth, avarice, gluttony, and lust. Furthermore, as we have seen, the first three form a group, as do the last three, with sloth or *acedia* located between the two groups. Are Thomas and Dante at odds here? One could say that Thomas provides us with a theoretical basis for the distinct capital sins, each of which gives rise to other sins (for example, the vices derived from pride), while the arrangement of the *Purgatorio* stresses the relations between the capital sins themselves. The root of them all is pride, which disposes to envy and anger; one is reminded of the Sartrean *mot*, "Hell is other people."[9] There is no division of opinion between Thomas and Dante as to the ordering of the capital sins that we find in the *Purgatorio*.

Mary and the Capital Sins

After ante-Purgatory, Dante and Virgil begin their laborious climb of the mountain, a climb that will become progressively less laborious as they ascend. The strains of "*Salve, Regina*," sung by the late repentant, come to them from below as they climb. Monks sang this antiphon each night after Compline as they went to their cells:

> Salve, Regina, Mater misericordiae;
>   vita, dulcedo et spes nostra, salve.
> Ad te clamamus, exsules filii Evae.
> Ad te suspiramus, gementes et flentes
>   in hac lacrimarum valle.
> Eia ergo, advocata nostra,

illos tuos misericordes oculos
ad nos converte.
Et Jesum, benedictum fructum ventris tui,
nobis, post hoc exsilium ostende.
O clemens, o pia, o dulcis Virgo Maria.

Hail holy Queen, mother of mercy, our life, our sweetness, and our
hope. To you do we cry, poor banished children of Eve. To you do
we send up our sighs, mourning and weeping in this vale of tears.
Turn then, most gracious advocate, your eyes of mercy toward us,
and after this exile show unto us the blessed fruit of thy womb Jesus.
O clement, O loving, O sweet virgin Mary.

Now night falls and all activity on the mountain ceases, so Dante
sleeps. When he awakes, in canto 9, he finds that he has been carried
in his sleep up to the gate of Purgatory; three steps lead to it, representing confession, contrition, and reparation.

The gatekeeper, reassured by the information that St. Lucy has
sent them, invites Dante to climb those three steps. That done, he
traces seven P's on Dante's forehead. The letter P is for *peccatum*, sin,
and the seven letters stand for the seven capital sins. The steps leading
to the gate are of different colors, suggestive of confession, contrition, and reparation; the gate itself is set on rock, the rock of Peter on
whom Christ has built his church. It opens, providing a narrow way
through, then shuts noisily behind Virgil and Dante. And then the
strains of "Te Deum laudamus" (*Purg.* 9.141) are heard.

Eight cantos were devoted to ante-Purgatory, nearly a fourth of
the cantica. Seven levels or terraces rise before Dante, each representing a capital sin, beginning with the most serious, pride, and ending
with the least serious, lust. A walkway encircles the mountain, rising as it does from level to level. Opposing each capital sin is one of
the beatitudes—Dante has need of only seven. The penitent endures
a particular penalty or punishment on each level and is instructed
not only by the relevant beatitude but, most importantly for our purposes, by examples of the virtue opposed to the vice being expiated.
And on every level, and in the first place, the example of the virtue is
drawn from the life of the Blessed Virgin.

Dante may have been influenced here by the *Speculum Beatae Mariae Virginis*, a medieval work attributed in his time to St. Bonaventure. Lectio 15 of the *Speculum* discusses the thesis, "That Mary is blessed with seven virtues opposed to the capital vices." The author is commenting on the angelic salutation, "Blessed art thou amongst women." Virtue makes one blessed or happy, and "Mary is blessed for her humility, which is opposed to pride; for her charity, which is opposed to envy; for her meekness, which is opposed to wrath; for her promptness, which is opposed to sloth; for her liberality, which is opposed to avarice; for her sobriety, which is opposed to gluttony; and for her chastity, which is opposed to lust."[10] Mary is thus a compendium of the Christian virtues, the highest created model.

The similarity between Dante's *Purgatorio* and this allegedly Bonaventurian work[11] is striking, but so are the differences. Dante, as we will see, always relies on the New Testament in calling attention to the appropriate virtue in the Blessed Virgin. *Speculum Beatae Mariae Virginis* always illustrates the virtue of Mary by finding it in some figure from the Old Testament who prefigures Mary. Speaking of her humility, for example, the *Speculum* author cites Psalm 118(119):21 and Isaiah 4 and then finds in Axa, in the Book of Judges, a figure of Mary.[12] In discussing Mary's charity, he appeals to Sarah; in discussing her promptness, which is opposed to sloth, he cites Genesis. The *Speculum* continues in this vein, relying on the Old Testament and the prefiguring of Mary in Old Testament women for an understanding of Mary's virtues. It is otherwise in the *Purgatorio*. What is common to the two treatments is that Mary is the embodiment of the virtues opposed to the seven capital sins. The difference lies in the scriptural examples.

Dante bases his presentation of Mary as the exemplar of each of the virtues opposed to the capital sins on the following biblical texts:

1. Luke 1:38 – humility as opposed to pride (*Purg.* 10.34–45)
2. John 2:1–11 – mercy or generosity as opposed to envy (*Purg.* 13.28–30)
3. Luke 2:41–46 – meekness as opposed to anger (*Purg.* 15.85–92)
4. Luke 1:39 – zeal as opposed to sloth (*Purg.* 18.97–100)
5. Luke 2:7 – poverty as opposed to avarice (*Purg.* 20.19–24)
6. John 2:1–11 – temperance as opposed to gluttony (*Purg.* 22.142–144)
7. Luke 1:34 – chastity as opposed to lust (*Purg.* 25.127–128)

Nel ciel dell'umiltà ov'è Maria: In the heaven of humility where Mary is

Dante and his guide find themselves on a narrow pathway winding round the mountain and without a guard rail. On this first level, where the sin of pride is expiated, they immediately come upon examples of humility, the virtue opposed to pride. Engraved in stone at their feet are figures so vivid that it is as if they can be heard as well as seen. The first example of humility is Mary, the Mother of Jesus, and the episode in her life chosen to convey this is the Annunciation.

The Annunciation, that fateful moment when the angel Gabriel came to Mary and greeted her with the salutation, "Hail Mary, full of grace, the Lord is with thee," is surely Dante's favorite scene. He came by it honestly, so to speak, for the Annunciation was a favorite subject of artists and painters, and Dante's theological guides—St. Bernard, St. Bonaventure, and Thomas Aquinas—loved to dwell on this scene and to draw from it all they could.

Bernard, for example, remarks on the specificity of the scene, the names and the place given. "Now in the sixth month the angel Gabriel was sent from God to a town of Galilee called Nazareth, to a virgin betrothed to a man named Joseph, of the House of David, and the virgin's name was Mary" (Luke 1:26–28). The sixth month of what? Of her cousin Elizabeth's pregnancy, of which we have just read in Luke. The rest of the passage imparts the full weight of history to this moment. It is God who sends his angel Gabriel to the Virgin Mary, who is betrothed to Joseph of the House of David. This links Mary to the whole history of Israel, the long preparation of the Jewish people for this moment when salvation is at hand. That history is present in its entirety to God. He has been guiding its temporal unfolding all along. The free acts of men and women, performed for purposes of their own and intelligible to them in the short term, become part of the divine plan to save his people. What God has planned cannot not come about, and yet he works through the free actions of men. This is a great mystery, one that has prompted the fruitful meditation of the Church fathers and theologians. Are our acts free or determined? They are free, but for all that they play a part in God's predestined plan. From all eternity Mary was chosen for this singular role, to be the mother of the Incarnate God, but she must freely accept her role. "When she had heard him she was troubled at his word, and kept pondering what manner of greeting this might be" (Luke 1:29). Gabriel understands. "Do not be afraid, Mary, for thou hast found grace with God. Behold thou shalt conceive in thy womb and shalt bring forth a son: and thou shalt call his name Jesus. He shall be great, and shall be called the Son of the Most High; and the Lord God will give him the throne of David his father, and he shall be king over the house of Jacob forever; and of his kingdom there shall be no end" (Luke 1:30–33).

Again, Luke reminds us of the genealogy of Mary and of her son to be. The long history of the human race has been gathering to this moment; this simple virgin at prayer is the means God has chosen from all eternity to save His people. He will come among us as one of us, human as well as divine, and for that he needs a mother. The scene could well have been the occasion to call attention to the way in which God humbles himself in the Incarnation. Who could be more humble than Jesus, who "though he was by nature God, did not consider being equal to God a thing to be clung to, but emptied himself, taking the nature of a slave and being made like unto men. And appearing in the form of man, he humbled himself, becoming obedient to death, even to death on a cross" (Phil. 2:6–8). The mother of such a son must herself be humble. "But Mary said to the angel, "How shall this happen, since I do not know man?" (Luke 1:34). Is this hesitation? Mary has to know to what she is giving her assent. She must take on her predestined role freely and consciously. To call her a virgin is not simply to note that she is *intacta*. According to long-standing Christian tradition, from this point on, if not before, she is a virgin by choice in order to more completely devote herself to God. Is that vow to be set aside?[13]

"And the angel answered and said to her, 'The Holy Spirit shall come upon thee and the power of the Most High shall overshadow thee; and therefore the Holy One to be born shall be called the Son of God'" (Luke 1:35). Mary will conceive in a miraculous way; her spouse will be the Holy Spirit, so her child will indeed be the Son of God.

There are angels and angels. The one who has come to Mary, in Christian tradition, is an archangel, in the highest tier of the hierarchy of angels. But even if we came down the angelic hierarchy to the least of angels, and there must be a least, we are still dealing with a creature whose natural perfection surpasses that of any human being to an unimaginable degree. An angel is a pure spirit. Its existence is not measured by time; its knowledge is infused into it, not gathered from experience. Thomas Aquinas structures the angelic hierarchy in terms of the number of ideas each angel needs in order to know what it knows. The more ideas required, the less perfect the angel and the more its knowledge approaches ours, so to speak; our ideas are formed on the basis of sense experience, wresting the natures of things from their singular circumstances. This abstracting takes time, based as it is on experience, and our thinking is sequential. Truths bring to light other truths. Call our knowledge discursive. But even the lowest angel knows with intuitive simplicity, compared to human knowledge. The gap between men and angels is all but infinite, though there is an analogy between them. And the Archangel Gabriel has been sent as a messenger to this virgin, scarcely more than a girl, inviting an assent on which the whole future of the world depends.

With angels as well as humans, we must distinguish the natural from the supernatural order. The Annunciation is the moment when the whole natural order is stood on its head. A simple little girl is to become the Mother of God and thereby first among all creatures in the supernatural order. However more perfect than Mary Gabriel naturally is, from the supernatural point of view she will become his queen. How could artists, poets, and theologians not ponder this scene and seek to draw from it all that it contains? "But Mary said, 'Behold the handmaid of the Lord; be it done to me according to thy word.' And the angel departed from her" (Luke 1:38). There it is, the hinge of the history of salvation which turns on the *fiat* of Mary.

Dante, seeing that scene inscribed in stone, hears, as it were, Mary's answer. "*Ecce ancilla Domini,*" behold the handmaid of the Lord.

> esser di marmo candido e addorno
> d'intagli sì, che non pur Policleto,
> ma la natura lì avrebbe scorno.
> L'angel che venne in terra col decreto
> de la molt' anni lagrimata pace,

ch'aperse il ciel del suo lungo divieto,
    dinanzi a noi pareva sì verace
quivi intagliato in an atto soave
che non sembiava imagine che tace.
    Giurato si saria ch'el dicesse 'Ave!';
perché iv' era imaginata quella
ch'ad aprir l'alto amor volse la chiave;
    e avea in atto impressa esta favella
'*Ecce ancilla Deï*', propriamente
come figura in cera si suggella.
                      (*Purg.* 10.31–45)

There in white marble, adorned with carvings beyond the skill not
only of Polycletus but of nature too, the angel who brought to earth
the decree of the peace tearfully longed for during all those years and
which opened the heavens so long closed, appeared before us, so truly
graven there in gracious attitude that it seemed an image that could
speak. One would have sworn that he said, "Ave!" for there was
imaged too she who turned the key that opened supreme love, and
her whole attitude expressed these words, "Behold the handmaid of
the Lord," as clearly as an image pressed in wax.

In humility the soul is emptied of all desires except to serve the
will of God. Before His will, one becomes as nothing. The example of
Mary etched in stone is followed by two others: David dancing before
the ark and the Emperor Trajan. In the example from the Old Testament, the psalmist David is Mary's ancestor and thus the ancestor of
Christ, but the other is taken from secular history. How could a pagan
emperor exemplify the Christian virtue of humility that is opposed to
pride? The scene depicted in stone focuses on a poor widow, who is
humbly begging a favor from Trajan. According to a story in the Middle Ages, St. Gregory brought the dead Roman emperor back from
hell and baptized him. We will meet Trajan again in the *Paradiso*.

    The action on this terrace has so far concentrated on humility as
the remedy for pride. That remedy is given pride of place. Now, having had the opportunity to ponder the scenes etched in stone, Virgil
draws Dante's attention to an approaching throng. We are about to

meet the proud who are atoning for their sin. Dante adopts an openly hortatory tone:

> Non vo' però, lettor, che tu ti smaghi
> di buon proponimento per udire
> come Dio vuol che 'l debito si paghi.
>   Non attender la forma del martìre:
> pensa la succession; pensa ch'al peggio
> oltre la gran sentenza non può ire.
>   (*Purg.* 10.106–111)

Reader, I would not weaken your resolve on hearing how God wills the debt be paid; do not dwell on the form of the punishment, think of what comes next, think that at worst it cannot go on beyond the great judgment.

Those who have been guilty of pride and vainglory atone for their sins by carrying huge boulders that all but flatten them to the ground. Once they looked with lifted chin on the world as their oyster; now they are as a pair of claws scuttling across the floor of unknown seas, weighted down so that their gaze is on the ground.

To impose such corporeal punishment on souls involves conceptual difficulties. How can a separated soul be oppressed by the weight of matter? Dante several times calls attention to the fact that, unlike Virgil and the others whom they meet, he alone casts a shadow and makes footprints. He is still a man, body and soul, but the souls of the departed no longer have a body. How can they be corporeally punished?

Although the literal meaning of the passage raises such difficulties, we have no trouble with its allegorical sense. Those who have lifted themselves up high must be brought low. And the desire for lowliness is simply a full realization of the fact that God is He Who is and we are his creatures, dependent for every moment of our existence on his sustaining will; comparatively speaking, we are nothing at all. In that humble realization our elevation becomes possible. Blessed are the meek, the humble, because their reward is the incomprehensible glory of the vision of God. Domenico Bassi comments,

Humility is the emptiness the soul makes in itself and of itself, in order that God might fill it; the proud consider themselves the proprietors of everything and lack that poverty that gives the right, so to speak, to the supreme richness. That is why Saint Augustine says that Mary was pleasing to God because of her virginity, but it was because of her humility that she conceived Him: *Virginitate placuit, humilitate concepit.*[14]

In the *Convivio* 4.5, Dante had already linked the Incarnation and the Roman Empire. The divine plan will come to fruition in the fullness of time; the world must be readied for the coming of the Son of God. That readiness on the political plane, he tells us, required that the whole earth be brought under one regime. The Rome founded after the long journey of Aeneas from Troy became the master of the known world:

E però che ne la sua venuta nel mondo, non solamente lo cielo, ma la terra convenia essere in ottima disposizione; e la ottima disposizione de la terra sia quando ella è monarchia, cioè tutta ad uno principe, come detto è di sopra; ordinato fu per lo divino provedimento quello popolo e quella cittade che ciò dovea compiere, cioè la gloriosa Roma.

But in order that at His coming into the world both heaven and earth might be in the best disposition, and the best disposition of the earth is when there is monarchy, that is, everyone under one prince, as was said above; divine providence ordained that that people and that city should accomplish this, that is, glorious Rome.

Rome, David, Mary—these three are linked by Dante as he reflects on the Annunciation.[15]

Vinum non habent: They have no wine

No images are inscribed on the livid pavement of the next terrace; where dwell the souls of the envious, for their eyes are sewn shut. The proud labored under weighty stones; the punishment of the envious is blindness. Dante and his guide climb to this second level to find seated figures. In life these souls saw the good that happened to others as a threat, and they wanted to confiscate it rather than rejoice in the happiness of others. Virgil has not been here before, of course; he is in as much need of guidance as Dante. We sense the gradual diminution of his initial role until, at the end of the ascent of the mountain, he will turn Dante over entirely to another. Virgil prays for help, and winged spirits appear. They are singing *"Vinum non habent"*: "They have no wine" (*Purg.* 13.29).

The words evoke the scene of Christ's first miracle, the wedding feast of Cana in John 2. (Like the Annunication, this event will twice provide examples of Mary's virtue.) The wedding feast is well under way, the guests have drunk to the happiness of the newlyweds with gusto, and the wine is running low. Mary goes to her Son and tells him, "They have no wine." The words emerge from her compassion for the couple; the prospect of empty glasses with nothing more to fill them will be an embarrassment and take some glow from the celebration. That is the sense of her remark to Jesus. Imagine how differently those words might be spoken by another, you or I perhaps, with a little lilt in the voice, widened eyes, lifted brows, calling attention to the impending embarrassment of the hosts.

Jesus's response to his Mother is noteworthy, and it might seem cold. "What is that to me and thee?" And, more significantly, "My hour has not yet come" (John 2:4). Jesus has yet to manifest his divinity by performing miracles, and we are invited to think that he intended to put that off to a later day. And now his mother has come to him, and he seems indifferent to the plight of the newlyweds. Mary knows better. She instructs the servants to do what Jesus tells them. At his direction they fill huge jars with water, which, when ladled up, turns out to be not merely wine but wine far better than had been served. And we are given the prudent judgment of the steward: One doesn't save the best wine until last but serves it first. Once the headiness of the best wine takes effect, a lesser vintage can be brought out. The miracle has reversed that order.

This first miracle of Jesus is prompted by his mother, as if her intercession suffices for him to change his mind. His hour has come after all. What has prompted Mary is the virtue opposed to envy. The envious would take wicked pleasure from the prospect of a wedding feast winding down because of the embarrassing fact that there is no more wine. How amusing. How fitting that the father of the bride, up to this point the beaming master of the revels, should be brought low by such a humiliation.

The virtuous response, in contrast, is one of sympathy, of sharing the possible pain of the givers of the feast, and of acting out of that sympathy. The good of others is to be rejoiced in; their evil is to be deplored and, if possible, alleviated. "They have no wine." In the *Paradiso* (33.16–18) we are told that Mary not only *responds* to our pleas for help but sometimes gives her help even *before* it is asked. That is surely the case here. No one has brought the problem to her, but she brings herself to the problem. One of the winged spirits in the *Purgatorio* adds another maxim to the mix: "Love thy enemies."

Atto dolce di madre: Sweet motherly deed

As Dante and his guide struggle through dark smoke to the third terrace of the mountain, the scene seems to be one from the *Inferno*. The air is acrid and gritty. Dante cannot see where they are going, and Virgil urges him to keep near lest they be separated. Dante follows as a blind man follows his guide.

The smarting smoke that envelops them represents the way in which wrath blinds us to the good. In the *Inferno* (8.42) one of the wrathful had tried to upset the little boat ferrying Dante and Virgil across the Styx, and Virgil had fended him off, crying, "Get out of here to the other dogs." The wrathful who are damned become dogs. In the *Purgatorio*, the effects of wrath are done away with by acquiring the meekness of the Lamb of God.

Dante and Virgil hear around them the voices of penitents singing the *Agnus Dei:* "Lamb of God, who takes away the sins of the world, have mercy on us." The singing of the *Agnus Dei* is part of the therapy of this level; it soothes savage breasts of the effects of sins of anger during their earthly lives. The mildness of the lamb is contrasted with the unbridled passion of the wrathful. The meekness of the lamb represents the virtue opposed to wrath. John the Baptist identified Jesus as the Lamb of God, and the preeminent model of what we are called to be is the Incarnate God.[16] Mothers sometimes teach their children a simple prayer: "Jesus meek and humble of heart, make my heart like unto thine." My own mother taught it to me, and in doing this she was playing a role not unlike that of the Blessed Mother. Naturally, we resist this ideal meekness, just as we resist the call to humility. All the capital sins are children of pride, and pride is resistance to our condition as creatures. Again, we see how the model of Christian perfection flies in the face of our human, all too human, self-assertion, and indeed is the very opposite of religion within the limits of reason alone.

Jesus, the lamb of God, presents himself as the sacrificial victim. He is the price of our salvation. Silent before unjust accusation, he willingly accepts the most ignominious of deaths in order to set us free from all the sins that chain us and separate us from the one thing needful. How does Mary exemplify meekness?

> Ivi me parve in una visïone
> estatica di sùbito esser tratto,
> e vedere in un tempio più persone;
>   e una donna, in su l'entrar, con atto
> dolce de madre dicer: "Figliuol mio,
> perché hai tu così verso noi fatto?
>   Ecco, dolenti, lo tuo padre e io
> ti cercavamo."
> (*Purg.* 15.85–92)

> There I seemed caught up in an ecstatic vision and saw many people
> in a temple, and a woman at the door who with the sweetness of a
> mother said, "My Son, why have you done this to us? Behold, your
> father and I have sought you sorrowing."

The loss of the child Jesus in the temple, referred to in these lines, is the third of the seven sorrows of the Blessed Virgin but the fifth joyful mystery of the rosary. The sorrow points to those dreadful three days during which Mary and Joseph sought their missing son, and the joyful mystery to the happy outcome when Jesus is discovered in the temple, astounding the elders with his interpretations of Scripture.

In this scene, Mary seems to be scolding Jesus, just as his response seems something less than filial; he chides her for spending three long sorrowful days searching for him. We might imagine Mary as more than annoyed, as angry. Yet Dante takes her reaction here to be a revelation of her meekness, *mansuetudo*. The sixteenth-century theologian Cornelius of Lapide warns us against the interpretation just given.

These words of his mother, Cornelius argues, are to be taken not as scolding him but rather as spoken in wonder and sorrow, to explain the sorrow of his parents to him. We are meant to see in Mary's words the veneration of the mother for such a son, namely, the God Man; thus it is likely, Cornelius reasons, that she spoke to him not publicly in the gathering of the elders but privately, either calling him from the gathering or waiting until after it had dispersed. And of course, Cornelius gives us the testimony of other scriptural exegetes to this effect.[17] He points out, moreover, that the acts of Christ are threefold: those that derive as such from his divinity, to create, preserve, and govern all things; those that derive from his humanity, such as eating and sleeping; and those that are a mixture of each, including teaching and performing miracles. Christ is subject to his parents in his purely human acts but not in the others, and that is the point of his reply to his mother.

St. Thomas considers clemency and meekness together. He distinguishes them by explaining clemency as the leniency of a superior toward an inferior, whereas meekness can be shown by anyone to anyone. In both cases they are the opposite of anger or the irascible. Meekness governs the desire for revenge, and clemency bears on penalties to be inflicted. Thus, Thomas opposes meekness to wrathfulness and clemency to cruelty. Now if meekness is the virtuous moderation of anger, the biblical passage on Mary's words in the temple suggests that although Mary mastered her annoyance, she nonetheless felt it.[18]

But surely, Thomas retorts, wrath or anger is not always a vice. In the *Disputed Questions on Evil* he invokes St. John Chrysostom, St. Paul, Gregory the Great, and the *Glossa Ordinaria* (a celebrated medieval commentary on Scripture) on behalf of justified anger. Meekness and clemency are treated in his *Summa theologiae* as parts of temperance, which governs our natural impulse to anger. Thomas recalls the ancient quarrel between Stoics and Aristotelians, the former treating all anger as a vice, whereas the latter held that sometimes anger is good. As a passion, anger has a formal and a material aspect. The formal aspect is the desire for revenge, the *appetitus vindictae*. The material aspect is the bodily disturbance—the rush of blood, the physical agitation. As a passion, anger is a sense appetite, something we experience willy-nilly in certain circumstances. But there is more in us than instinct, the mindless response to our circumstances. Our will enters in, and with it reason or intellect, and then our action—for now, by involving reason and will, it is *our* action, a conscious human act and not merely an event that happens to us—will be either good or bad.

> For it is obvious that when someone seeks recompense according to the ordered requirement of justice, this is a virtue; for example, when punishment is required as correction to sin, the right order being observed; and this is to be wrathful toward sin. However, when one seeks vengeance but not in an ordered way, it is a sin, either when one seeks more than justice requires, or intends the extermination of the sinner rather than the abolition of sin. (*De malo*, q. 12, a. 1)

Given these distinctions, Thomas concludes that there is no difference between the Stoic and the Aristotelian, since the Stoic too must hold that there is justifiable anger. The Stoic, noting that passion often impedes reason, judges that what is material in anger, the instinctive reaction that must be directed by reason, is defective as such. In short, all anger would be a vice. But surely this is wrong:

> Because man's nature is composed of soul and body and of an intellectual and sensitive nature, it pertains to the good of man that his whole self be subject to virtue, that is, his mind, sensitive part, and body; therefore the virtue of man requires that the fitting desire for revenge be not solely in the rational soul, but also in the sensitive part and in the body too, and the body is moved to serve virtue. (Ibid.)

Furthermore, the Stoic should consider that passion relates to reason diversely, sometimes antecedently, sometimes consequently. In the first sense, it sweeps reason along, and this is scarcely virtuous, whereas in the second sense, as following on reason, passion is at the service of the rational judgment, and is virtuous. Indeed, it helps enact the judgment of reason.

"Your father and I have sought you sorrowing." The sorrow that Mary naturally feels at the loss of her Son is subsumed by the virtue of meekness.

Maria corse con fretta a la montagna: Mary ran with haste to the mountain

As we have seen, the sin of sloth is represented on the terrace that separates the three below it from the three above. Only one canto is devoted to the capital sin of sloth and its opposed virtue. Dante and Virgil, after a discussion of free will—actually, the second installment of it—come upon the penitents of this level. (The discussions of free will are undertaken lest the assumptions of the Christian vocation, and of the *Comedy*, be undermined.) The rushing band of souls working off the lingering stain of sloth cry out, as they approach:

> Tosto fur sovr' a noi, perché correndo
> si movea tutta quella turba magna;
> e due dinanzi gridavan piangendo:
> "Maria corse con fretta a la montagna";
> (*Purg.* 18.97–100)

There soon drew near a great crowd on the run and two of them, weeping, cried out, "Mary ran with haste to the mountain."

The reference is to the account in Luke of the angel's visit to Mary. Part of Gabriel's annunciation to Mary was that her cousin Elizabeth was also with child, whereupon Mary set off straightway to visit her and hurried up the mountain to the city of Judea. The promptness of Mary's act makes it a model of zeal, the virtue opposed to the vice of sloth:

Now in those days Mary arose and went with haste into the hill country, to a town of Juda. And she entered the house of Zachary and saluted Elizabeth. And it came to pass, when Elizabeth heard the greeting of Mary, that the babe in her womb leapt. And Elizabeth was filled with the Holy Spirit and cried out with a loud voice saying, "Blessed art thou amongst women and blessed is the fruit of thy womb. And how have I deserved that the mother of my Lord should come to me? For behold, the moment that the sound of thy greeting came to my ears, the babe in my womb leapt for joy. And blessed is she who has believed, because the things promised her by the Lord shall be accomplished." (Luke 1:39–45)

We may pause a moment here to reflect, has any other part of Scripture had a more enduring and pervasive effect on the Church's liturgy than the first chapter of Luke? The joyful mysteries of the rosary take us through it again and again. And of course the Angelus prayer recapitulates the Annunciation scene: "Angelus Domini annuntiavit Mariae; et concepit de Spiritu Sancto" (The angel of the Lord declared unto Mary and she conceived of the Holy Spirit). This is followed by an *Ave Maria*, then "Ecce ancilla domini; fiat mihi secundum verbum tuum" (Behold the handmaid of the Lord, be it done unto me according to thy word). Another *Ave Maria*, then "Verbum caro factum est, et habitavit in nobis" (The Word was made flesh and dwelled amongst us). *Ave Maria*, then "Ora pro nobis, Sancta Dei Genetrix, ut digni efficiamur promissionibus Christi" (Pray for us O holy Mother of God, that we may be made worthy of the promises of Christ).

Cornelius of Lapide, in his discussion of Luke, provides examples of what the fathers and doctors of the Church have said on the passage describing Mary's visit to Elizabeth. "In those days" is interpreted to mean that this event took place the day after the Annunciation. And why did Mary go? Cornelius gives four reasons. First, in order that the Word conceived within her might be announced to others and his grace communicated to them; in short, she wanted Christ to begin his office of Savior, the reason for his coming, even while he was still in her womb. St. Ambrose (as cited by Cornelius) adds that she did not go out of disbelief that her aged cousin was pregnant, nor because she doubted the news the angel had given her. Second, the visit had the intention of absolving Elizabeth's child, John the Baptist, of original sin. Third, the visit was to help the older woman. And,

Fourth, that she might give to all future ages a striking example of humility and charity, by which, now made Mother of God and queen of the world, she deigned to go to Elizabeth who should more properly have tended to and served her, in order that we too should follow her example and willingly visit the poor and those beneath us, in order to cheer them and brace up their souls.[19]

St. Ambrose (as cited by Cornelius) has this to say about the phrase that Dante stresses—she ran *con fretta*, with haste. A first reason for haste is lest she be outside her home too long and be delayed in public; Ambrose invokes an admonition to virgins not to dwell in the piazza or chat with others. Another and perhaps more persuasive reason is that, full of the joy of the Holy Spirit, she was prompted by it to hurry to her cousin.

Is sloth simply laziness, tepidity, lack of promptitude? That is its obvious meaning, and the one that shines forth in canto 18, whose opposite is exemplified by the immediacy of Mary's response to the angelic news that her cousin was with child. But that does not exhaust the meaning of this vice. Psalm 90(91) was once invoked in exploring those further meanings, and verses 3–6 could be found in the pre–Vatican II Latin breviary as follows:

3.   For he has freed me from the hunter's snare, and from the bitter word.
4.   You will be protected by his shoulders and will hope beneath his wings.
5.   You will be protected by the shield of his truth: nor will you fear the terror of the night,
6.   or the arrow that flies in the daytime, neither the pestilence hidden in shadows nor the attack of the noonday devil (*daemonio meridiano*).[20]

The *daemonio meridiano* in verse 6, translated as the noonday devil, has disappeared from the current breviary and, indeed, he never made it into either the Rheims-Douay or the King James Bibles, which have "the destruction that lays waste at noonday" and "the destruction that wasteth at noonday," respectively. What was the noonday devil supposed to be? Andrew Greeley, in reviewing for the *New York Times* a novel of mine with that title, remarks that in the seminary they were taught that this devil is lust. There is not a perfect identification of lust with sloth, but *acedia* or sloth, as we shall see, is connected with sins of the flesh.

St. Thomas describes sloth, like envy, as opposed to the joy of charity; it is opposed to the divine good, just as envy is opposed to the good of one's neighbor. It is an aggravated sadness that impedes action. The slothful are frigid, frozen in inactivity; they are those for whom all is tedium.

> This kind of sadness is always an evil; sometimes just as such, sometimes because of its effect. That sadness is as such evil which bears on something apparently evil but truly good, just as conversely evil delight is of the truly evil and only apparently good. Since spiritual good is the true good, sadness with respect to spiritual good is per se evil. But that sadness too which is of what is truly evil can be evil in its effect, and thus it agitates a man such that he totally withdraws from good works; hence the Apostle (2 Cor. 2:7) does not want any penitent to be absorbed by too great a sadness because of sin. Therefore, acedia as understood here signifies spiritual sadness and is twice evil, in itself and in its effect. (*ST* IIaIIae, q. 35, a. 1)

Since any sin can be said to involve sadness about some spiritual good, according to Thomas, it may seem that *acedia* cannot be a special vice. Nor can we simply say that such sadness comes into play because a spiritual good is difficult or entails bodily discomfort incompatible with sensual pleasure. That would be true of any carnal vice. What is necessary to understanding sloth is the recognition that there is an order of spiritual goods, with the divine good being chief among them. The special virtue of charity bears on the divine good, and charity brings with it a joy in the divine good. Thus, although any sin entails sadness with respect to a spiritual good, sadness as to the acts consequent upon charity gives rise to the special vice of *acedia* (*ST* IIaIIae, q. 35, a. 2). This justifies calling *acedia* a capital sin, since just as the delights of all the virtues are ordered to that of charity, similarly, sadness about the latter gives rise to other and lesser sadnesses (a. 4). Thus, one who feels sadness with respect to spiritual goods is led on to carnal activities: the pursuit of pleasure in the usual sense stems from fleeing the greatest spiritual good, the *gaudium caritatis* or joy of charity (a. 4, ad 2).

> Spiritual goods, which sadden the one in the grip of *acedia*, are both ends and means. Flight from the end is caused by despair, whereas flight from the means to the end, insofar as they are arduous and come under counsel, is caused by pusillanimity; with respect to what pertains to common justice, it is caused by torpor about the precepts. The belligerence of those saddened by spiritual goods sometimes is directed against those who urge us to spiritual goods, and one comes to detest them, and this is properly malice. However, insofar as one is led by sadness in face of spiritual goods to external pleasures, a daughter of *acedia* is "flight to the illicit." (*ST* IIaIIae, q. 35, a. 4, ad 3)

(These daughters of *acedia* also enable Thomas to accommodate remarks of Gregory the Great and Isidore about the various defects in monastic life: idleness, somnolence, curiosity, verbosity, restlessness, and instability.)

Dante would have been aware of these refinements of the notion of sloth. Without them, we would be tempted to think of it as mere sluggishness or laziness—on the order of "Oh, how I hate to get up in the morning, O how I hate to get out of bed" in objection to those whose kinetic energy keeps them bouncing around. These further reflections are essential if we are to understand sloth as a capital sin, as in Dante, and not merely as the opposite of feverish activity.

Non erat eis locus in deversorio: There was no room in the inn

Unlike the descent through the Inferno, which was accomplished in a single day, the ascent of Mount Purgatory takes several days, and given days, several nights, nights during which Dante sleeps. All activity ceases during the night there, but only Dante is in need of sleep. This calls attention to his anomalous presence in the other world; he is a man of flesh and blood, his feet make impressions when he walks, his body casts a shadow, and with the onset of night he requires sleep. To sleep, perchance to dream. Canto 19 of the *Purgatorio* opens with an account of a dream Dante had while he slept. An ugly woman appears to him, but she gradually becomes attractive and announces that she is the Siren whose seductive song has led so many mariners to their doom.

When I was in the Marine Corps boot camp long ago, we were shown various films, some of them having to do with the perils of liberty—in the military sense. In one of them, the actor Robert Benchley, improbably attired in uniform, enters a bar, orders a drink, and notices an ugly woman several stools away. He turns from her to his drink. He goes on drinking. When he looks at the woman after a passage of time, she is transformed, and her ugliness has given way to a seductive beauty. There is no need to dwell on the sequel and the lesson the film was meant to teach. Something like this takes place in Dante's dream, but the seductive role is played not by alcohol but by concupiscence. A lot of space is accorded to this dream, and it can be regarded as the prelude to the three capital sins yet to be dealt with: avarice, gluttony, and lust. "Love calls us to the things of this world," the poet Richard Wilbur wrote. Dante would doubtless want to substitute "concupiscence" for "love" in that sentence.

Domenico Bassi connects Dante's dream to St. Paul in Romans 13, where Paul gives expression to a thought that rules the *Comedy*: "Let every soul be subject to the higher authorities, for there exists no authority except from God, and those that exist are appointed by God. Therefore he who resists the authority, resists the ordinance of God; and they that resist bring on themselves condemnation" (Rom. 13:1–2). Then, having listed some of the commandments one must observe—Do not commit adultery, Do not kill, Do not steal—Paul likens ignoring them to living in a dream:

> And this do, understanding the time, for it is now the hour for us to rise from sleep, for now our salvation is nearer than when we came to believe. The night is far advanced; the day is at hand. Let us therefore lay aside the works of darkness, and put on the armor of light. Let us walk becomingly as in the day, not in revelry and drunkenness, not in debauchery and wantonness, not in strife and jealousy. But put on the Lord Jesus Christ, and as for the flesh, take no thought for its lusts. (Rom. 13:11–13)

Preferring temporal to eternal goods might be a definition of the sins on the upper three terraces of Mount Purgatory. Material possessions, food and drink, and venereal pleasure are all good things, but they are good for us only insofar as they are integrated into our comprehensive good. When we try to make them serve as the be-all and end-all of life, when they become our gods—St. Paul said of the glutton, "whose god is his belly"—our actions are sinful. This is the explanation of the upper three terraces that Virgil, when he was explaining the geography of Purgatory to Dante, promised to give later.

If we had to come up with a symbolic figure of avarice, we might think of Midas, or Dickens's Scrooge, or the miser in Balzac's *Eugenie Grandet* running his greedy fingers through his gold. Dante puts before us numerous examples including a French king and a pope, choices with obvious political ramifications. Dante lamented that popes had betrayed the Church by their avarice, yet he also laments the French king who assaulted Pope Boniface VIII at Anagni, a pope Dante excoriated as a person; but it is the papal office he defends here.

Such figures represent the vice; Mary represents the opposite of avarice, that is, poverty. Dante has in mind Luke's account of Christ's birth.

> Now it came to pass in those days, that a decree went out from Caesar Augustus that a census of the whole world should be taken. This first census took place while Cyrinus was governor of Syria. And all were going, each to his own town, to register. And Joseph also went from Galilee out of the town of Nazareth into Judea to the town of David, which is called Bethlehem—because he was of the house and family of David—to register, together with Mary his espoused wife who was with child. And it came to pass while they were there, that the days for her to be delivered were fulfilled. And she brought forth her firstborn son, and wrapped him in swaddling clothes, and laid him in a manger, because there was no room for them in the inn. (Luke 2:1–7)

Penitents invoke this scriptural passage to contrast their own sins with the poverty of the Blessed Virgin:

Noi andavam con passi lenti e scarsi,
e io attento a l'ombre, ch'i' sentia
pietosamente piangere et lagnarsi;
    e per ventura udi' "Dolce Maria!"
dinanzi a noi chiamar così nel pianto
come fa donna che in parturir sia;
    e seguitar: "Povera fosti tanto,
quanto veder si può per quello ospizio
dove sponesti il tuo portato santo."
                            (*Purg.* 20.16–24)

With slow and short steps we went on, and I was intent on the shades,
hearing their pitiful weeping and lamenting, when I chanced to hear
one ahead of us call tearfully, "Sweet Mary!" sounding like a woman
who is giving birth, and he went on, "How poor you were can be seen
from that inn in which you laid down your holy burden."

The penitents cry out to Sweet Mary, whose poverty was manifest
at the nativity when she had nowhere to lay her newborn son but in a
manger. Many have seen in this passage the powerful influence on Dante
of St. Francis of Assisi—Dante himself was a member of the Franciscan
Third Order, a lay order. Poverty, one of the three vows of the religious
life, along with chastity and obedience, was often more honored in the
breach than in the observance. The Franciscan order had lifted poverty
to new heights. The voluntary turning away from possessions and from
the goods of this world was the soul's opening to the eternal.

The *contemptus mundi* that had been urged upon members of religious orders, and not only on them, could be distorted into a devalu-
ation of the created order, as if lesser goods were not goods at all. Here
we find the seeming paradox of St. Francis. In embracing Lady Poverty
he turned his back on lesser goods, but at the same time he became the
poet of nature, expressing our kinship with every living thing. This is an
ordered love of the things of this world. In Francis's words, "Benedicite
omnia opera Domini Domino"—Blessed by the Lord are all the works
of the Lord. What we call the necessities of life are just that; we cannot
live without them. Food and drink may be lesser goods, but we need
them to survive, just as the species needs the sexual drive to replenish

itself. Franciscan poverty draws attention in a dramatic way to the fact that the pursuit of lesser goods must be ordered.

Those doing penance for avarice on Mount Purgatory lie face down—"My soul is prostrate in the dust" (Ps. 118[119]:25)—symbolizing a disordered attachment to wealth and to the things of this world. Dante understands the temptation to which those doing penance here have succumbed. He is not merely a spectator, nor are we meant to be. In other works, such as the *Convivio* and his letters, he confesses listening to the siren song that promised wealth, pleasures, and all the rest. Is it only because he never attained wealth that he can see how incommensurable it is to man's desire for the good? That would be a cynical conclusion. Thomas Aquinas did hold, however, that the best argument against the belief that such goods as wealth, food, and pleasure are able to fulfill our heart's desire is to have had them. Dante has certainly known many pleasures, and they are dust and ashes. Vanity of vanities, all is vanity, to quote Ecclesiastes. And to call this thought a leitmotif of the Psalms would be an understatement: "Lo, thou has made my days but a span, and what is the length of my days, and my life is as nothing before thee; every man is but a breath. Man passes away like a mere shadow, his worrying is all in vain, he gathers up and knows not who shall reap" (Ps. 38[39]:67). Some vices attract an individual more than others; in contrast to other vices, Dante gave short shrift to *acedia*, a vice to which apparently he was never tempted.

At this point in the cantica the Roman poet Statius appears. The five hundred years he has spent on this terrace are over. His release has been signaled by a quaking of the mountain and shouts of thanksgiving and singing of the *Gloria in excelsis Deo*, but he lingers to speak with these two strange pilgrims. He is, it emerges, an admirer of Virgil; his own epics were inspired by the *Aeneid*. All this bursts forth before Statius realizes that Dante's guide is Virgil himself. At that, he kneels to kiss the hem of the great poet's garment but is prevented by Virgil. We are thus given yet another indication of why Virgil was chosen by Beatrice for the role he plays in the *Comedy*.

We now have three poets, Virgil, Dante, and Statius, and they will soon speak with other poets, contemporaries of Dante. We shall return later to the suite of cantos called the cantos of the poets. For now, we have Statius's testimony to Virgil that the great epic poet was the cause of Statius's conversion to Christianity. As if wishing to cover for the fact that there is no historical basis for this conversion, Dante presents Statius as a secret Christian, one who sympathized with the martyrs who were led into the Coliseum but could not bring himself to join them. Virgil's role in his conversion is linked to Virgil's fourth Eclogue, in which, to the early Church, the pagan poet had seemed to prophesy the coming of Christ. Thus the effect of Virgil on Statius was twofold—thanks to Virgil, Statius has become first a poet and then a Christian. Virgil is portrayed as a guide who held a lamp behind him, lighting for others a way he did not go himself.

Why did Statius have to repent for five hundred years on the terrace of the avaricious? Virtue is a *via media*, flanked by opposite vices, and the vice opposite to avarice is prodigality, a mindless stewardship of worldly goods. That was Statius's vice. Virgil tells Statius of all the great poets confined in Limbo, to which he himself must return, and the three continue together and are soon on the next terrace.

Nondum venit hora mea: My hour is not yet come

The sixth terrace is the one on which sins of gluttony are repented. For Mary as an example of the opposite virtue, Dante returns once more to the account of the wedding feast at Cana found in the Gospel of John. Earlier, he had found in Mary's behavior compassion for their hosts, who were running out of wine. Now he finds another significance in her prompting Her Son to perform his first public miracle.

As the three poets walk, they come upon a tree with sweet-smelling fruit. It is a tree of curious shape, like an upside-down fir tree, perhaps to prevent its being climbed. As they approach, a voice warns them not to eat of this tree. We are reminded of the Tree of the Knowledge of Good and Evil in Eden, but the voice continues:

> Poi disse: "Più pensava Maria onde
> fosser le nozze orrevoli e intere,
> ch'a la sua bocca . . .
> 			(*Purg.* 22.142–144)

> Then it said, "Mary thought more that the wedding feast should be honorable and complete than of her own hunger."

Mary's concern is the success of the wedding celebration rather than filling her mouth. It was not a desire for more to drink that prompted her. Chiavacci Leonardi finds this a somewhat forced use of the text, commenting that "the paucity of evangelical texts that speak of Mary offered little choice."[21] One might rather say that a surprising number of texts mention Mary, but perhaps that would seem forced in its turn. Dante also might have chosen his example from the Magnificat: "the hungry he has filled with good things and the rich he has sent away empty."

Because of the pleasure associated with eating and drinking, whose objects are necessary if we are to live, the rational moderation of them can be difficult. One cannot swear off drinking except in the sense of drinking certain beverages or too much of a certain kind of beverage, but beverage we must have. The fact that rational control of such activities can be difficult, given their centrality in our lives, explains why sin often occurs as we engage in them.[22] Gluttony is the immoderate desire for food, not just the consumption of it. One might very well take more than one needs under the assumption that it is as much as one needs, and this would not be gluttony. Imagine some new and exotic food about whose effects one is unaware, such that a little bit counts as a lot. Gluttony proper is the *desire* for an immoderate amount, followed for the most part by eating an immoderate amount, but the latter is consequent on the former. When it is not, as in the example suggested, there is no gluttony. Nor is there any constant objective measure of too much or too little; this varies from person to person, and each must moderate his desire according to his disposition. A fighter in training will need more food than the reporter reporting on him. Morever, gluttony can be a venial, not a mortal sin. It is a capital sin insofar as the immoderate desire for food becomes one's defining goal, one's ultimate end: *cuius deus venter est.*

We notice, once again, that the objects of the capital sins that are expiated on the top three levels of Purgatory bear on things— possessions, money; food and drink; sexual activity. None of these objects is evil in itself; indeed, each in its way is necessary for human beings. Capital sins arise from the immoderate desire for these objects, elevating a particular good into the overwhelming rationale for our deeds, and the fact that such immoderate desire gives birth to other faults.

Those doing penance for gluttony are portrayed as an anorexic band, tormented by hunger and thirst and with barely enough flesh on their bones. This suggests perhaps the vice opposed to gluttony: as prodigality relates to avarice, so we might say that dieting relates to gluttony. Dieting, that is, in the sense of a deliberate denial of food and drink related not to the first good, or rational moderation, but to another lesser good—the dream of slimness, wellness, rippling middle-aged muscles, and all the fads that would seem to amount to desperate efforts to drive out thoughts of ageing and mortality. The mirror on my lady's table, called ominously a vanity, is perhaps an innocent version of this. Who has not felt a foolish pleasure in being told he looks younger than he is, as if somehow the common lot of shuffling visibly toward the end had been abrogated for us, while others, sans hair, sans teeth, sans everything, visibly age. Think of the manic joggers, the desperate devils on their treadmills, those whose glowing flesh is acquired in tanning parlors, face lifts, liposuction, and so on. Is there not excess in this? But of course, another vanity is in noticing this, possibly a version of *acedia*. Between the obesity consequent on gluttony and the painfully acquired svelteness that is the opposite vice resides the virtue of temperance. And here, as always, Mary is the first exemplar of the virtue.

Virum non cognosco: I know not man

And so we arrive at the seventh and last terrace, devoted to atoning for sins of lust. Before the travelers encounter any souls on this terrace, however, Dante takes up a question, the answer to which has been assumed all along. In the *Inferno*, in the moving encounter with Paolo and Francesca, the doomed lovers are locked in an eternal embrace. At the time Dante did not ask how souls can embrace, nor did the deeper issues of how souls can suffer the quite physical pains of hell (or purgatory) detain him. Now, before the last step of emerging from the uppermost terrace of the seven storey mountain, the question is at last posed.

Several times along the way, mention had been made of the fact that Dante makes footprints and casts a shadow. The shades he meets do not. Are they simply separated souls? If so, what explains the seeming bodies, shapes, voices, and the rest? Is that to be taken as merely imaginary, a poetic necessity? Canto 25 gives Dante's answer, which deserves at least brief mention. Virgil turns the question over to Statius, who provides a lengthy resumé of the Aristotelian embryology that was taken over by medievals such as St. Thomas Aquinas. In this account the embryo is not human until God breathes a soul into it. There are profound problems associated with such a theory of postponed animation, but those problems will not detain us now. What is important is that Statius, in his account of the development of the now human embryo, refers to the formation of a first spectral body before the actual, physical body is complete, as if the soul, now animating the embryo, first produces the plan of the physical body that later will form. This may seem an idle point, until we consider the state of the soul after death. And that is Dante's problem, as it has been from the outset. He must attempt to answer such questions as: How can the souls of the departed be affected by physical punishment? How can they suffer from fire, for example? And how can they grow thin, as with the emaciated shades on the previous terrace who are expiating for gluttony? His solution is that a spectral body accompanies the soul after death. Hence the departed are visible to Dante, not merely as a poetic device but in reality. As Chiavacci Leonardi suggests, we do not find in Dante the merely separated soul, that is, the "form" of the body released from the body and now quite independent of it. The departed for Dante are not soul and physical body, as on earth, but soul and spectral body. (As she also points out, this is one of the most extended and self-contained theoretical passages in the entire cantica.)

Fire did not play a central role in Dante's depiction of the torments of the damned, nor has it figured in the purgations of the previous terraces. Now the travelers see the souls of the lustful being purged by fire. From the depths of the fire, Dante hears voices singing

"Summae Deus clementïae" (*Purg.* 25.121), "God of supreme clemency," which, as Dante commentators point out, is from the hymn sung at Matins on Saturdays. The chief relevance of its appearance here may perhaps be found in the third stanza:

> Our reins and hearts in pity heal,
> And with the chastening fires anneal;
> Gird thou our loins, each passion quell.
> And every harmful lust expel.[23]

Dante sees spirits walking in the flames; they are singing the hymn, and when they finish they cry aloud, "Virum non cognosco," I know not man. This of course was Mary's reply to the angel when he told her she was to become a mother. Taken as a vow to chastity, how can what the angel tells her come about without abandoning that vow? The answer is that she will conceive in a wholly miraculous way, be at once both virgin and mother. The spirits then begin the hymn again, in lower voices. Once more, the Annunciation as recounted in Luke is invoked to show Mary as the prime example of purity.

Dante turns now to the lustful sinners. They are of two groups, those who sinned unnaturally and those who sinned naturally; a division, that is, between homosexuality, on the one hand, and fornication and adultery, on the other.

We live in a sensate age in which it is often said that the sense of sin has been lost. Certainly there has been an enormous change as to how, in the modern world, the pleasures of the flesh are regarded. There has always been a willingness to regard sins of the flesh as less than serious. How else explain the long puzzlement over Paolo and Francesca? Is a little hanky-panky really deserving of an eternal punishment? Dante occupies a world that will seem incredible to those for whom sex is merely an innocent conjunction, for recreation, not procreation, an end in itself. Let us state the most obvious difference between such an attitude and the one that Dante represents. The point of the division of the species into genders, male and female, is that families may be formed and children conceived, nourished, reared, and educated in everything a person needs before launching out on his or her own. Sex and procreation imply sex and marriage.

Dante's early poetry dwelled on love, but it was an asexual love and whatever else he came to find wanting in it, he would not have regarded such poetry as a celebration of illicit love, that is, physical love outside matrimony.

Christianity has always been countercultural, however much at times this seems muted, as if some detente had been achieved between believers and the world. Believers who take seriously the Catholic Church's reminders about the main truths of sexual morality will realize how out of step the Church and they are with the way we live now. For the Catholic doctrine on the basis of sexual morality, we can consult St. Thomas's *Disputed Questions on Evil*.

Lust, for Thomas, is the vice opposed to temperance that moderates the pleasures of touch and sex, just as gluttony is opposed to the moderation of concupiscence with respect to food and drink. Lust is primarily, then, a want of ordering, a disorder.

This disorder may be either in the interior passions or in exterior acts that are of themselves disordered, and not disordered simply because they come from disordered passions. Thomas invokes the parallel case of greed or avarice. A man might desire in a disordered way the acquisition of money; there is nothing wrong per se with acquiring money, but the passion with which one goes about it can be disordered. How so? Because wealth is the avaricious person's overriding objective; it is a lesser good put over the higher. Sometimes avarice not only may consist of disordered desire but may also bear on an act that is objectively disordered, such as stealing another person's goods. Such a one is doubly at fault; both the disordered passion and the objectively disordered act are contrary to liberality and constitutive of illiberality. It can be much the same with lust.

One might have a disordered passion and engage in an act that is of itself legitimate, such as sleeping with one's spouse. But even the conjugal act can be vitiated by lust. The marriage licence is not a licence to licentiousness and orgy. Once this might have been difficult to acknowledge, but no one can now deny that a man can rape his wife or that a woman could force her husband against his wishes. Again, this is a double fault, inner and outer. But some acts are objectively wrong and are not made wrong merely because of the disordered passion with which they are undertaken; in Thomas's words, "as happens in every use of the genital members outside the marriage act" (*De malo*, q. 15). That every such act is disordered in itself is clear from the fact that every human act is disordered when it is not proportioned to its proper end. Similarly, eating that is not proportioned to bodily health, to which it is ordered as to its end, is disordered. "The end of the use of the genital members is generation and any use which is not proportioned to the generation of a child and of the upbringing due it is of itself disordered." This is why it is disordered for an unmarried couple to engage in the sexual act, whether one or both are married to someone else or not. The reproductive system is ordered to reproducing; the sexual act is the way this is done; to engage in coition humanly is to be aware that a child may result and that one has obligations to that child which will extend over many years. Any sex act outside of marriage is objectively disordered.[24]

At the time Thomas wrote, and before and after, it was doubtless true that many behaved in ways contrary to the truths he expounds. Sexual morality has doubtless always been observed more in the breach than in the observance. Our times seem different because now theories are advanced for what hitherto was recognized as wrong behavior. It is as if the other sins to which our flesh is heir were to have theoretical advocates, with the formation of communities of thieves, of murderers, or of liars, proudly proclaiming their own right to behave as they do. Because the sexual drive is fierce and fundamental, ordered as it is to the propagation of the species, it is subject to frequent deviant uses.

It is not, of course, my intention here to enter further into these controversies. Suffice it to say that Dante would have accepted without demur Thomas's position, as is evident in his treatment of adultery and homosexuality in the *Inferno* as well as in the penance done for sins against lust in the *Purgatorio*, and this despite the fact that he apparently strayed from time to time in matters of the flesh. He was more interested in repenting of his sins than seeking to justify them. When Our Lady appeared in the twentieth century at Fatima, the heart of her message was the need for purity and chastity. She was addressing our times. She would lead us out of the dark wood of our sins, much as she led Dante.

Dante and the Poets

Already in the *Vita Nuova* we find our author to be a highly self-conscious poet, much given to comparing his own efforts with those of others. Teodolinda Barolini[25] has tracked the way in which, in the course of his writings, Dante provides little lists giving the pecking order of contemporary poetic greatness; she even provides a helpful chart of these orderings. Poets to whom Dante at one time defers later fall back on his lists, or are even dropped altogether. Guido Cavalcanti is a dramatic example. In Dante's *Rime* he occupies pride of place in a list that includes Lapo (Lippo; probably the minor poet Lippo Pasci d'Bardi), with Dante modestly coming in third. Cavalcanti retains this prominence in the *Vita Nuova,* but he fails to show up in similar rankings in the *Convivio* and *Monarchia.* He is reduced to tangential references in the *Comedy,* once in the *Inferno* and once in the *Purgatorio.* Such shifts and altered estimates can be discussed in terms of poetic craft and the "sweet new style" of which Dante finally emerges as the master. But the discussion of the poets in the *Purgatorio* suggests that something deeper is at work, something more essentially related to the great aim of the *Comedy*—to lead us from the misery of sin to eternal bliss.

Starting with the appearance of Statius in canto 21, we have a suite of cantos that have been called the cantos of the poets. Our original duo is now joined by Statius. Dante depicts himself as following after Virgil and Statius, listening to them discourse on poetry and learning as he listens. When Statius realizes that he is confronted by the great epic poet of the founding of Rome and of the eclogue taken to be a prophecy of the Incarnation, he is as overwhelmed as Dante was at the outset of the *Comedy.* He details the effect that Virgil had on him and declares, in summary, "Per te poeta fui, per te cristiano" (*Purg.* 22.73): "you made me both a poet and a Christian."

George Santayana, in his marvelous little book *Three Philosophical Poets,*[26] refers to Lucretius as the poet of naturalism, Goethe as the poet of romanticism, and Dante as the poet of the supernatural. Santayana groups all three together under the rubric "philosophical poets." There is warrant for this homogenization, but in the case of Dante it is inadequate. Christianity is not a philosophy. Dante would better be called a theological poet, although his assimilation of Aristotle and others gives him claim to the title of philosophical poet as well. This brings us to a theme I touched on earlier and to which I promised to return.

In the *Republic*, Plato describes an ancient quarrel between the philosopher, of which he is one, and the poet and gives the basis for the quarrel. But it will occur to any reader of Plato that his philosophical dialogues are also works of art. Indeed, when Aristotle mentions the types of poetry in his *Poetics*, he lists the Platonic dialogues as one of them. Elsewhere, with reference to the Platonic notion of participation, Aristotle dismisses it as a mere metaphor, and the metaphor is the mark of the poet. This is rather a criticism of a transgression of genera than hostility toward poetry. The ability to see similarities in dissimilar things is the genius of the poet, and the metaphor is the vehicle of that vision. We expect Aristotle to ponder formal differences between kinds of discourse, including the nature of that nonpoetic discourse called philosophy. Aristotle's answer is laid out for us schematically by Thomas Aquinas in the preface to his commentary on Aristotle's *Posterior Analytics*.[27] In developing these thoughts here, I am providing something more than deep background for understanding Dante. The aim is to become clear as to what kind of poet Dante was, in terms of the philosophical tradition in which he stood.

The human mind forms its ideas on the basis of sense experience and then fashions affirmations and denials, which are the loci of truth—and of its opposite, of course. Affirmations are true when they capture the ways things are, and false when they fail in this. Progress occurs here, namely, discourse, the movement from one known thing to another, but discourse in the richer sense occurs when we arrive at new truths from old: that is, when we move from the fact that certain propositions are true to conclude that something else is true because of them, derivatively. This discourse, or syllogism, is the mark of our rationality. It is also a sign that while human reason is the most perfect thing in the physical cosmos, it is the lowest kind of intelligence in the universe. Despite the great gap between us and the angels, Thomas loves to speak of human reason as the bottom rung of a hierarchy that goes up through the progressively more perfect intellects of the angels to God himself. Putting human reason in its place is by no means to devalue it as such. Indeed, human rationality is the basis on which we can extrapolate to other forms of understanding that are not hampered in the ways ours is.

According to Thomas, Aristotle was the first to lay out the formal logic of the syllogism, in the *Prior Analytics*. There the topic is the relationship between symbols rather than what they symbolize. If A is B and B is C, then A is C. This formality of discourse proliferates into the figures and modes of syllogism. Aristotle's *Posterior Analytics* turns from the symbols to the symbolized. There is a necessity of consequence in the formal syllogism, but not everything we reason about is in fact necessary. The necessary is that which cannot be otherwise, and there are interpreted symbols that yield necessary conclusions, not just the necessity of consequence.

In explicating Aristotle, Thomas has begun to lay out for us the cascading types of discourse, from necessary arguments, through probable or likely reasoning, through persuasive discourse, and then, after a treatment of how arguments go wrong (fallacies), poetic discourse. The last type, he tells us here, as he had in the *Summa theologiae*, is *infima doctrina*, "the least of doctrines"—the bottom rung of human discourse. By the representations he or she puts before us, the poet leads our mind onward. My love is like a red red rose. Shall I compare thee to a summer's day? We are a little world made cunningly.

This cascade from apodictic through probable and forensic discourse to poetic discourse may seem to us to be a great put-down of poetry. It is better to think of it as the comparative location of poetry. Anyone familiar with the *Poetics* will know that Aristotle is fully aware of the power and range of the poetic. The point of any hierarchy is not that anything less then the first is to be ignored, but that we not confuse the lesser with the higher. Those in the Aristotelian tradition put apodictic discourse first, but not everything lends itself to such discourse; indeed, in a sense, few things do. Most of our arguments are probable to one degree or another; most of the truths we hold are only opinions. The mark of the wise man, Aristotle noted, is to demand and expect of a subject matter only the degree of rigor it can deliver. If we demanded mathematical rigor of every argument, we would be sorely disappointed. Think of any political dispute. Think of arguments in a court room. The primacy of apodictic discourse begins to look like a reminder of how rare it is. Against this reminder, we are less likely to think that calling poetic discourse *infima doctrina* is a way of saying, "Away with the poet!" We need poetry just as, in general, we need art. It is worth remembering that Aristotle must have seen a lot of plays in order to write as he did of Greek tragedy.

Poetry is an imitation, Aristotle stated; art imitates nature. This is not a plea for photographic realism. The *Poetics* has come down to us as a fragment; it gives us an analysis of tragedy. The tragic drama is an imitation in that it puts before us characters who act in much the way that members of the audience have acted and do or will act. But the imitation gives us a *logos*, a sense of wholeness, that ordinary life seldom does. In Aristotle's pithy phrase, the plot, the logos of the drama, has a beginning, a middle, and an end.

When Thomas says that poetic discourse is *infima doctrina* in the *Summa*, it is in the context of noticing that Scripture is replete with images and similes and parables. The problem this poses is the following: if sacred doctrine is the most sublime, why does it so constantly, almost exclusively, use poetic language and metaphors? Consider that the metaphors of the poet illumine that which is less than human by attributing human attributes to it—smiling meadows, and the like. Some metaphors go in the opposite direction, but they can be considered parasitic on the first kind. The point of scriptural metaphors, Thomas argues, is to give us forceful presentations that speak of God in human and even subhuman terms—he is a father, he repents of creating man, he is a fire, he is a lion, and so forth. Such metaphors proportion the divine to us in a way that is far more effective than abstract characterizations of him.

> It is fitting that Sacred Scripture should treat of divine and spiritual things as similar to the corporeal. God provides for things according to their natures, and it is natural to man that he should move to understanding from the sensible, since all our knowledge takes its rise from the senses. Thus it is that Sacred Scripture fittingly presents spiritual things to us by way of bodily metaphors. (*ST* Ia, q. 1, a. 9)

Thomas adds that Scripture addresses all people, both the wise and the simple, and thus speaks of spiritual things under bodily similitudes that all can grasp and that the wise, too, need.

He further contrasts the aim of the poet and that of Scripture. The poet makes use of representations because they are pleasing to us, generating the shock of recognition, the inner Aha! we feel at the fittingness of a metaphor. Scripture, on the other hand, uses metaphors out of necessity and usefulness. Of course, a literal understanding of Scriptural metaphors would defeat their purpose and lead to an inappropriate view of God. This is not a great danger, since everyone, wise and simple, has the hang of metaphors. The very reach of the metaphors that present God to us have a built-in caveat that we are learning what God is not rather than what he is.

On Santayana's account of the philosophical poet, a philosophy—such as naturalism, romanticism, and supernaturalism—gives us a view of the whole, and the philosopher has appropriate modes of argumentation to establish that vision. From the philosophical poet we do not expect philosophical arguments, but rather we expect the assumption of the vision that the philosopher *argues* for, as the background for poetic representation. Santayana makes a good case for this, and he is followed in it by his student T. S. Eliot, in Eliot's lectures on the metaphysical poets. One might demur, at least in part, by pointing to versified philosophical arguments in Lucretius and Dante, but by and large it seems a convincing account, with interesting implications for Dante's claim that the *Comedy* is an instance of moral philosophy. More interesting still, perhaps, is to compare the poetic expression of philosophical claims in the *Comedy* with more prosaic expressions of them elsewhere. Examples would be a comparison of Dante's embryology, presented by Statius, with the Aristotelian texts on which it is based, or of Dante's account of spectral bodies with the texts of Thomas on which it is based.

In the doctrinal cantos devoted to the problem of love and freedom in the *Purgatorio*—there are three—the doctrine that love is at the source of all eventually raised the question as to whether we act freely, once love has come. As we saw earlier, Dante once held this deterministic view. He now frees himself from it and has Virgil refer to the error of the blind who had posed as his guides (*Purg.* 18.18).

Recall again the beginning of the *Comedy*, when Dante is in the dark wood, in danger of losing his soul, and the long journey before him is the path of salvation. But Dante is a poet, and his presence in that dark wood is at least in part due to his poetic activity. What he now undertakes, as pilgrim and poet, is the story of his progressive assimilation of the Christian vocation.

The highest terrace of the upper three of the seven storey mountain concerns lust, which, like avarice and gluttony, puts a lesser good in the place of the highest good. The discussion of poetry through these terraces must accordingly bear on the way in which the poet can mistake a lesser good for the highest good. The great subject of the poetry of the other poets encountered was love, and presumably a lesser love that was treated as the dominant point of human life. It is this assumption of his own early poetry that Dante repents. Under the influence of Virgil and Statius, he now strives not only for a new poetic style but for one appropriate to singing of the love that moves the sun and other stars, and of life as the pursuit of that love. In his commentaries on the poems in the *Vita Nuova* he attempts to sublimate his love for Beatrice, but after her death he lived a life that was enveloped by a dark wood, in which the right path was lost. At the end of the *Vita*, Dante acknowledges his dissatisfaction with what he has written of Beatrice and resolves to devote himself to the study of philosophy and theology in order to write of her as no woman has ever been written of before. The *Comedy* is the fulfillment of that resolution. In it, Beatrice is the representative of true beatitude and Dante's guide, at first mediated but finally direct, leading him to a happiness that can only be found in the next world. Dante became not only a philosophical poet but, far more importantly, a theological poet. The preeminence that Dante claims over poets contemporary with him is precisely that his poetry is now at the service of Love in the most exalted sense.[28]

The writer François Mauriac, who was stung by the shocked reaction of fellow Catholics (as well as by André Gide's jibe that he sought permission to publish so he wouldn't have to burn his books), entertained misgivings about his novels. Would it be too much to suggest that Dante's allusions in the *Comedy* to his earlier works, those that shared the outlook of his fellow poets, convey a similar judgment? In any case, Dante came to view his earlier poetic practice as harmful to the writer, as the "cantos of the poets" in the *Purgatorio* suggest.

The subject of art and morality is usually discussed with reference to the effect of works of art on the reader. It is intriguing to find the artist worrying about that, but also worrying about the effect of what he has written on himself. Is it a repentant poet who is speaking to us in these cantos of the *Purgatorio*? Of course, it is not poetry as such that Dante abjures. He is now engaged in the kind of poetry that is both fulfilling of the writer and edifying to the reader. For dramatic contrast, all one need do is compare the Lord Byron of *Don Juan* with this learned, mystic, serious poet on his way to heaven, and hoping to take us with him.

Salire a le stelle: To climb unto the stars

Dante, persuaded to enter the fire in which certain poets and those guilty of lust in the usual senses burn, and reassured by Virgil that beyond the fire he will be reunited with Beatrice, soon finds himself in the earthly paradise, the garden of Eden, located at the very apex of the mountain. Earlier he had dreamed of Leah and Rachel, and in the garden he is met by a mysterious woman, Matilda, who sings beautifully. She represents, it would seem, the natural happiness for which man was originally destined. All that was changed by sin, and the remedy is the redemption and the promise of a happiness far above that proportioned to human nature. Hence the Augustinian description of original sin, *O felix culpa*, since what was lost is as nothing to what can be gained. Paradise lost is paradise regained, perhaps, but the meaning of "paradise" has changed. And then, in canto 30, a veiled Beatrice appears, and Dante turns to find that Virgil is no longer at his side.

The garden functions as a reminder of the vast difference between the natural and the supernatural. Virgil, as the representative of the natural, gives way to Beatrice, having fulfilled the commission he had accepted from Beatrice when, prompted by St. Lucy, who was prompted in turn by Mary, she came to him in Limbo. One misses some acknowledgment here of what the great poet has done, some gesture of gratitude from Beatrice. But although Dante weeps at his disappearance, her present concern is to remind Dante of the transgressions for which his ascent of Mount Purgatory has been necessary. Earlier, Virgil gave what turns out to be his farewell address:

> . . . "Il temporal foco e l'etterno
> veduto hai, figlio; e se' venuto in parte
> dov' io per me più oltre non discerno.
>
> Tratto t'ho qui con ingegno e con arte;
> lo tuo piacere omai prendi per duce;
> fuor se' de l'erte vie, fuor se' de l'arte.
>
> Vedi lo sol che 'n fronte ti riluce;
> vedi l'erbette, i fiori e li arbuscelli
> che qui la terra sol da sé produce.
>
> Mentre che vegnan lieti li occhi belli
> che, lagrimando, a te venir mi fenno,
> seder ti puoi e puoi andar tra elli.
>
> Non aspettar mio dir più né mio cenno;
> libero, dritto e sano è tuo arbitrio,
> e fallo fora non fare a suo senno:
>   per ch'io te sovra te corono e mitrio."
>   (*Purg.* 27.127–142)

Son, you've seen the temporal and eternal fire and reached the place where my discernment fails. I have led you here through wit and art. Now let pleasure be your guide, for you are past the narrow paths. See the sun that on you shines, look at the grass, the flowers, the shrubs to which earth here gives birth. Walk among them as you await those happy loving eyes that wept when she chose me for your guide. You will get no further word nor sign from me, your will is free, right, and sane, and it would be wrong to act against it. Accordingly I place the crown and miter on you.

All the capital *P*'s have been erased from Dante's forehead, but his ordeal is not yet over. Beatrice confronts him with his misbehavior with the *pargoletta*, that slip of a girl (*Purg.* 31.59), who represents, it seems, more than one companion in dalliance after Beatrice's death. And so Dante stands, head bowed like a schoolboy, being scolded by his beloved. Beatrice is no longer one mortal woman in competition with others, but the means of Dante's salvation. To interpret her initial address to Dante as that of a woman scorned, if only posthumously, would be to miss the whole point of the *Comedy*. Sins are an offense against God and even when forgiven and atoned for, their memory remains. That is why Dante must be submerged in the water of Lethe by Matilda. This will be followed by a further bathing in the waters of Eunoe, which prepares him for the last leg of his journey. The Blessed Virgin is not mentioned in these final cantos of the *Purgatorio*, but none of this would have happened without her initial compassion for the Dante who had gotten himself into that dark wood.

Beatrice appears to be identified with Mary in the last cantos of the *Purgatorio*, or perhaps better, becomes an allegorical figure of Mary. Far more important, however, is the relationship between the first woman, resident of the Garden of Eden, and Mary.

Eva/Ave

There is something geographically odd about finding the Garden of Eden on top of Mount Purgatory. The explanation given is that the mountain was formed when Lucifer plunged into the earth, burrowing to its very center (the lowest circle of hell), and as he did so, pushing an equal volume of dirt out the other side, thus forming Mount Purgatory. The significance of the Garden is its role now, as Dante, his soul purged of the stain of the capital sins, comes onto the final stage of the cantica.

The drama of the *Commedia*, the whole drama of human life, began in that garden where our first parents, Adam and Eve, lured by the promise that they would be as gods if they disobeyed God, were driven from the earthly paradise into an unfriendly world where they and their progeny had to earn their bread by the sweat of their brow. Original sin is that great aboriginal catastrophe, as John Henry Newman called it, of which we all have some intimation in trying to understand why we and others act in the wrong and terrible ways we do.[29] Adam and Eve at their creation were untroubled by the division we are all too aware of in ourselves, with desire contesting with reason, so that we do what we should not and do not do what we should. How our first parents could have sinned, given their condition and what theologians call their preternatural gifts, is a problem which, like that of how angels could sin, we must set aside. (Beatrice, in her professorial mode, will discuss the angels, good and bad, in *Paradiso* 29.) If Adam and Eve had not sinned, human history would have been wholly different. We can lament that fact, but at the same time we must acknowledge with St. Augustine that the remedy for what was lost by original sin is more than compensation for it. A Savior would be sent, the very Son of God, who would reconcile the human race with the Father. Through him, we would be raised, not just to the status that was lost, but beyond it, to a supernatural life with the promise that we will see God even as we are seen.

In the *Paradiso* 7, we are given the essence of the matter when Beatrice explains Justinian's remark that the death of Christ was the vengeance of God.

> Solo il peccato è quel che la disfranca,
> e falla dissimìle al sommo bene,
> per che del lume suo poco s'imbianca;
>
>   e in sua dignità mai non rivene,
> se non rïempie, dove colpa vòta,
> contra mal dilettar con giuste pene.
>
>   Vostra natura, quando peccò *tota*
> nel seme suo, da queste dignitadi,
> come di paradiso, fu remota;
>
>   né ricovrar potiensi, se tu badi
> ben sottilmente, per alcuna via,
> sanza passar per un di questi guadi:
>
>   o che Dio solo per sua cortesia
> dimesso avesse, o che l'uom per sé isso
> avesse sodisfatto a sua follia.
>
>   Ficca mo l'occhio per entro l'abisso
> de l'etterno consiglio, quanto puoi

al mio parlar distrettamente fisso.
    Non potea l'uomo ne' termini suoi
mai sodisfar, per non potere ir giuso
con umiltate obedïendo poi,
    quanto disobediendo intese ir suso;
e questa è la cagion per che l'uom fue
da poter sodisfar per sé dischiuoso.
    Dunque a Dio convenia con le vie sue
riparar l'omo a sua intera vita,
dico con l'una, o ver con amendue.
    Ma perché l'ovra tanto è più gradita
da l'operante, quanto più appresenta
de la bontà del core ond' ell' è uscita,
    la divina bontà, che 'l mondo imprenta,
di proceder per tutte le sue vie
a rilevarvi suso, fu contenta.
    Né tra l'ultima notte e 'l primo die
sì alto o sì magnifico processo,
o per l'una o per l'altra, fu o fie:
    ché più largo fu Dio a dar sé stesso
per far l'uom sufficiente a rilevarsi,
che s'elli avesse sol da sé dimesso;
    e tutti li altri modi erano scarsi
a la giustizia, se 'l Figliuol di Dio
non fosse umilïato ad incarnarsi.

                                    (*Par.* 7.79–120)

In Allen Mandelbaum's translation,

    Only man's sin annuls man's liberty,
    makes him unlike the Highest Good, so that,
    in him, the brightness of Its light is dimmed;
        and man cannot regain his dignity
    unless, where sin left emptiness, man fills
    that void with just amends for evil pleasure.
        For when your nature sinned so totally
    within its seed, then, from these dignities,

just as from Paradise, that nature parted;
   and they could never be regained—if you
consider carefully—by any way
that did not pass across one of these fords:
   either through nothing other than His mercy,
God had to pardon man, or of himself
man had to proffer payment for his folly.
   Now fix your eyes on the profundity
of the Eternal Counsel; heed as closely
as you are able to, my reasoning.
   Man, in his limits, could not recompense;
for no obedience, no humility,
he offered later could have been so deep
   that it could match the heights he meant to reach
through disobedience; man lacked the power
to offer satisfaction by himself
   Thus there was need for God, through His own ways,
to bring man back to life intact—I mean
by one way or by both. But since a deed
   pleases its doer more, the more it shows
the goodness of the heart from which it springs,
the Godly Goodness that imprints the world
   was happy to proceed through both its ways
to raise you up again. Nor has there been,
nor will there be, between the final night
   and the first day, a chain of actions so
lofty and so magnificent as He
enacted when He followed His two ways;
   for God showed greater generosity
in giving His own self that man might be
able to rise, than if He simply pardoned;
   for every other means fell short of justice,
except the way whereby the Son of God
humbled Himself when he became incarnate.[30]

The means chosen, the Incarnate God, requires a mother, and this puts Mary in the very center of the divine plan.

Original sin can make it look as if God's plan was disrupted by Adam and Eve, requiring him to rewrite the script and introduce ad hoc adjustments. It is impossible for us not to think in this way. But God's plan did not change. From all eternity, he foresaw original sin and how he would remedy it. He created Eve to be the mother of us all, alas, a sinful mother. The Savior who would come, the God Man, would be born of a human mother, and that mother too was foreseen from all eternity. Her role as the mother of us all on the supernatural level was part of the single divine plan. In order for her to fill that role perfectly, she would be the most perfect of pure creatures, full of grace, of whom it can be truly said that she is the mother of God: "Vergine madre, figlia del suo figlio" (Virgin mother, daughter of your Son [*Par.* 33.1]). Unless we recognize, with Dante, that Mary is the most perfect of creatures, the mother of the savior, who interceded for us with him—as at the wedding feast of Cana; who dispenses grace surprisingly—as with the deathbed repentant, Buonconte; who was assumed into heaven, where, body and soul, she reigns as queen —unless these simple truths are truths for us, we will never fully appreciate Dante's attitude toward Mary and her role in the *Commedia*. Mary is not merely another human being, a very holy human being; she is the mother of God, and her maternity is by no means confined to an event in a cave in Bethlehem long ago. She is the new Eve, the mother of us all. Nor may we think that this status is something that we confer on her by our devotion. Her privileges come from God. Her supereminent role in the economy of salvation is part of God's plan, not a human construct.

The earthly paradise at the top of Mount Purgatory is portrayed in all its natural beauty, but it is empty except for the woman Matilda. Dante, seeing the setting in which an unfallen mankind had been meant to dwell, becomes indignant with Eve. Except for her sin and Adam's, he would have known these delights long since and for a longer time. But all this will seem as nothing when Dante is taken on to the paradise of the new dispensation by Beatrice.

The reunion of Dante and Beatrice is surprising. First of all, Dante experiences the reaction of a lover: "I felt the mighty power of old love" (*Purg.* 33.39). He borrows the line from Virgil's *Aeneid*, in which Aeneas's backward glance as he sails away from Dido prompts him to say, "I recognize the signs of an old flame." Beatrice's reaction is surprisingly different. As we have seen, she scolds him, intent on eliciting his shame for his conduct after her death, his fickleness, and in any other poem, with any other couple, this might be taken to be the pique of a woman scorned. But the shame Beatrice wants Dante to feel—she addresses him somewhat abruptly as "Dante" (*Purg.* 30.55)—is for turning away from from the object to which his love for her was meant to lead him. Beatrice's attendants ask why she shames her old lover so, and she answers at length:

> Alcun tempo il sostenni col mio volto:
> mostrando li occhi giovanetti a lui,
> meco il menava in dritta parte vòlto.
>   Sì tosto come in su la soglia fui
> di mia seconda etade e mutai vita,
> questi si tolse a me, e diessi altrui.
>   Quando di carne a spirto era salita
> e bellezza e virtù cresciuta m'era,
> fu' io a lui men cara e men gradita;
>   e volse i passi suoi per via non vera,
> imagini di ben seguendo false,
> che nulla promession rendono intera.
>   Né l'impetrare ispirazion mi valse,
> con le quali e in sogno e altrimenti
> lo rivocai: sì poco a lui ne calse!
>   (*Purg.* 30.121–135)

> My countenance sustained him for a while;
> showing my youthful eyes to him, I led
> him with me toward the way of righteousness.
>   As soon as I, upon the threshold of
> my second age, had changed my life, he took
> himself away from me and followed after
>   another; when from flesh to spirit, I
> had risen, and my goodness and my beauty
> had grown, I was less dear to him, less welcome:
>   he turned his footsteps toward an untrue path;

he followed counterfeits of goodness, which
will never pay in full what they have promised.
    Nor did the inspirations I received—
and which, in dreams and otherwise, I called
him back—help me; he paid so little heed.
                        (trans. Mandelbaum)[31]

In short, we are given a reprise of the whole basis for Dante's journey. He had sunk so low that the only means of bringing him back was to show him the horrors of hell and the pains of purgatory. In recounting how she went down to the gateway of the dead to provide Dante with the guide who has brought him at last to her, Beatrice makes no mention of her need to be prompted by St. Lucy, who had been stirred to action by the Blessed Virgin, but the reader will remember the ultimate aegis under which everything is taking place.

Between the earthly paradise and the ascent to Paradise, history intervenes: Dante puts before us a complicated pageant, rich with allegory, summing up the history of mankind and the plight that he judges the Church to be in. Having been chided like a schoolboy and reduced to tears for his sins, Dante is ready to drink from the rivers of Lethe and Eunoe, after which "I was pure and prepared to climb unto the stars" (*Purg.* 33.145, trans. Mandelbaum).

FOUR

Queen of Heaven

L'ombra del beato regno: The shadow of the blessed realm

In the final cantica of the *Commedia*, Beatrice and Dante fall upward, as it were. The highest good draws them magnetically—*gravitas* defies gravity—because of Beatrice's sanctity and the purging of Dante that has taken place as he clambered up Mount Purgatory.

How could any poet depict in words and their accompanying images what escapes all sensible representation? Dante seems to have assigned himself an impossible task. One solution is to call attention to the difficulty and, by addressing it, resolve it if only obliquely. But how does one express the ineffable except by words? Even "inexpressible" is a word. And our language comes trailing its origins in our sense experience. Take any word that is applied to an immaterial reality, let alone to God: it has been drawn from its native habitat, the realm of things proportionate to our knowledge, and made to serve a higher purpose than thinking and talking about the changeable things of this world. *Soul*? Its original meaning is breath, wind. *Father, good, one, intelligent, powerful, actual*—the entire vocabulary of the theologian is anchored, one way or another, in the sensible world. This extrapolation of words, this extension of their meaning, is justified because the sensible world is a sign of and a means of knowing its cause. In this sense, the very means that Dante uses, namely language, contains the solution of his dilemma.

It is not surprising, therefore, that Dante employs the planets of our system to represent degrees of beatitude. Beatrice will fly him to the moon and then to Mercury and all the rest, until, beyond these wheeling spheres, they reach the celestial empyrean, which is wholly immaterial and thus not a place. On the upward journey, during layovers on the various planets, Dante encounters the souls of the blessed, first those of the least degree and then upward through more intense participation in the divine goodness. No soul regards its measure of happiness as inadequate; even if it is aware of the greater beatitude of other souls, it has no desire for more. We can compare this to glasses of different capacity, each full to the brim. But although the various spheres and their differing proximity from the fixed stars provide a means for Dante to represent degrees of beatitude, we should not conclude that some blessed souls are caught up in the lunar sphere, others in the sphere of Mercury, Venus, and so on. The physical hierarchy of planets represents a spiritual hierarchy.

The ascending scale of blessedness is as follows: represented on the moon—although all the blessed are actually in the celestial rose— are those who were inconstant in vows; on Mercury, those who were ambitious in the active life; on Venus, the great lovers; on the Sun, the great theologians and other teachers; on Mars, the warriors; on Jupiter, the just; on Saturn, the contemplatives; in the heaven of the fixed stars, Dante will witness the triumph of Christ, the Virgin Mary, and will meet Adam and saints Peter, James, and John. In the ninth heaven Dante has a vision of the angelic hierarchy and then, in the tenth heaven, the empyrean, a vision of the celestial rose, the dwelling place of all the blessed, which is presided over by Mary, the Queen of Heaven. Only by images and words whose origins are in our common experience could Dante put before our eyes what cannot be seen and utter the ineffable.

The reader is permitted to think of this ascension, this astral journey, in more or less literal terms. After all, Dante still has a body, even if he needs no space suit or other provisions for an atmosphere different from the terrestrial. But we are given two precious downward glimpses as Dante and his beloved soar upward, first in *Paradiso* 22:

> Col viso ritornai per tutte quante
> le sette spere, e vidi questo globo
> tal, ch'io sorrisi del suo vil sembiante;
>   e quel consiglio per migliore approbo
> che l'ha per meno; e chi ad altro pensa
> chiamar si puote veramente probo.
>
> (*Par.* 22.133–138)

My eyes returned through all those seven spheres and I saw this globe in such a way that I smiled at its sorry appearance; I endorse that judgment as best which holds it least, and one whose thoughts go elsewhere can truly be called virtuous.

The second downward look, in canto 27, also conveys the modesty of earth among the swirling planets. If the earth is the center in this view of the planets, if geocentrism holds, yet that centrality does not grant it prominence. A reader who has been struck by the prescience of the air flight to Rome in Robert Hugh Benson's 1903 novel *Lord of the World* will be all the more awed by Dante's anticipation of today's marvelous photographs of earth taken from outer space. Such a small thing. And yet it is central in another way: earth is where men live and where the drama of their salvation was enacted. Dante's reader can never be so starstruck as to forget this.

Mane e sera: Morning and evening

The Blesssed Virgin may seem to be absent from the first two-thirds of the *Paradiso*, but to think so would be to forget the goal toward which Dante and Beatrice are rising. In canto 23, Christ and His mother become central. It is fitting that we enter upon what will prove to be a cumulative concentration on Mary by noting the role of Dante's personal devotion to her, which complements the recognition of the universal role of the Mother of God.

Il nome del bel fior ch'io sempre invoco
e mane e sera, tutto mi ristrinse
l'animo ad avvisar lo maggior foco.
                                  (*Par.* 23.88–90)

The name of that beautiful flower that every morning and evening
I invoke, drew my entire soul and reminded me of the greater focus.

This passage is not the sole instance of Dante's devotion and piety.[1] In a narrow sense of the term "autobiographical," this is the only explicitly autobiographical reference to Dante's spiritual life in the *Comedy*. But to suggest that only here can we discern Dante's personal devotion to Mary would be akin to concluding that since Dante is addressed by name only once, by Beatrice in canto 30 of the *Purgatorio*, we are in some doubt as to the identity of the narrator of the poem. For all that, this explicit reference to daily Marian devotions is a charming revelation; we think of Dante at dawn and dusk, *e mane e sera*, invoking Mary's protection during his day and night. Did he perhaps recite the Angelus?[2] It is appealing to think so, since that prayer lingers over the words spoken by Gabriel and Mary at the Annunciation. We should not overrate the significance of *e mane et sera*, but we should not underrate it, either. It is a memorable statement of Dante's devotion to the Blessed Mother.

After *Paradiso* 23 we come to the three cantos where Dante will confess his faith, express his hope, and declare his love. But first, let us consider the setting of canto 23. Dante and Beatrice have come up through the seven spheres of the planets and have arrived at the eighth heaven, the sphere of the fixed stars. There are two heavens above this realm, but they, unlike the planetary spheres and the heaven of the fixed stars, are invisible. In short, with the heaven of the fixed stars we have reached the boundary between the visible and invisible. Along the way, Dante and Beatrice have met with representatives of the enormous number of the blessed, whose true "location" is the celestial empyrean, heaven proper, which is beyond any reference to astronomical place. Almost immediately, Dante notices the expression of intense expectancy on Beatrice's face. The opening lines of canto 23 liken her attitude to that of a mother bird just before daylight.

Come l'augello, intra l'amate fronde,
posato al nido de' suoi dolci nati
la notte che le cose ci nasconde,
   che, per veder li aspetti disïati
e per trovar lo cibo onde li pasca,
in che gravi labor li sono aggrati,
   previene il tempo in su aperta frasca,
e con ardente affetto il sole aspetta,
fiso guardando pur che l'alba nasca;
   così la donna mïa stava eretta
e attenta . . .

(Par. 23.1–11)

Like a mother bird who has rested with her dear little ones among the branches during the night that hides all things, eager to see her longed-for chicks again and find food with which to feed them, a heavy task that pleases her, she awaits the sun with ardent love, waiting for dawn to break—so did my lady stand tall and watchful.

Beatrice tells Dante that what appears before them are the troops of the triumphant Christ. A description of Beatrice's expectant face continues, but then the sun appears, brighter than a thousand lamps that draw their light from that sun. Dante is beholding the Wisdom and Power, the one who opened the longed-for path between earth and heaven. The canto continues with Dante's description of his defective memory of this moment, and of the continuing difficulty of describing such indescribable things: "And thus, in representing Paradise, the sacred poem has to jump across, as does a man who finds his path cut off" (*Par.* 23.61–63). Dante is recalled from such ruminations by Beatrice.

   "Perché la faccia mia sì t'innamora,
che tu non ti rivolgi al bel giardino
che sotto i raggi di Cristo s'infiora?
   Quivi è la rosa in che 'l verbo divino
carne si fece; quivi son li gigli
al cui odor si prese il buon cammino."

(Par. 23.70–75)

"Why are you so fascinated with my face that you do not turn and look at the beautiful garden flourishing under the sun of Christ? There is the Rose in which the divine word became flesh, and the scent of lilies that enable men to find the right path."

Christ's entry into the poem is accompanied by that of His Mother. The blessed are depicted as a garden irradiated by the light of Christ, and chief among those flowers is Mary, the mystical rose, the mother of God. She *is* the celestial rose. Now Dante sees a torch-like light descend and form a crown like a ring, a garland revolving around Mary. It is an angel, the angel of the Annunciation.

> "Io sono amore angelico, che giro
> l'alta letizia che spira nel ventre
> che fu albergo del nostro disiro;
>   e girerommi, donna del ciel, mentre
> che seguirai tuo figlio, e farai dia
> più la spera supprema perché lì entre."
> *(Par.* 23.103–108)

I am the angelic love who turns about that exalted happiness that breathes from the womb where dwelt our Desire; so shall I circle, Lady of Heaven, until, following your Son, you have made that sphere yet more divine by entering it.

At this, all the blessed sing out the name of Mary as Christ and His mother rise triumphantly, and Dante is made aware of the deep affection all of them have for Mary. The blessed then burst into the song "*Regina celi,*" the antiphon of Eastertide:

Regina coeli, laetare, alleluia!
Quia quem meruisti portare
Resurrexit, sicut dixit, alleluia!

Queen of heaven, rejoice, alleleuia! Because He whom you merited to bear has risen as he said he would, alleluia![3]

The tenderness of the song, Dante tells us, was such that the memory of it never left him.

The ascension of Christ and Mary is preparation for what is to come, a foretaste of the culminating vision that will be granted later to Dante when he is taken up to the ninth and tenth heavens by Beatrice. But first he must undergo an examination in the theological virtues. Meanwhile, his appetite has been whetted by his vision of the triumphant Christ:

> Quivi trïunfa, sotto l'alto Filio
> di Dio e di Maria, di sua vittoria,
> e con l'antico e col novo concilio,
>   colui che tien le chiavi di tal gloria.
>   (*Par.* 23.136–139)

> Here, just below the high Son of God and Mary, he who is the
> keeper of the keys to glory triumphs in his victory together with
> the ancient and new councils.

This concluding reference to St. Peter, keeper of the keys, draws attention to the fact that the assembly of the blessed represents the Church Triumphant under the leadership of Peter. St. Peter will play a central role in the next canto.

If we look back on the opening lines of canto 23, the description of the mother bird anxious about her young, we see an inescapable reference to Mary. It is bracketed by the closing image of the throng of the blessed, lifting their arms longingly to her as she ascends. Dante compares them to an infant who, just after having been fed, extends its arms to its mother. The deep affection of all the blessed for Mary is filial.

Io credo in uno Dio: I believe in one God

In canto 24, Beatrice presents Dante to the assembled spirits. She notes that he is still in an earthly condition but is to be given a foretaste of the banquet that is their eternal sustenance. At this, a spirit detaches himself from the rest, and Beatrice identifies him as St. Peter. Beatrice asks Peter to test Dante's faith.

This canto and the two following it have often been compared to an academic examination and are called the doctrinal cantos. St. Peter examines Dante on the theology of faith, St. James on the theology of hope, and St. John on the theology of love. But what we are given is both like and unlike an exchange between master and pupil, at least if this is understood as an abstract and impersonal presentation of a subject matter. What we witness, and what is elicited from Dante by his three apostolic interlocutors, are professions of faith, of hope, and of love. Here Dante lays bare what governs his life, the three theological virtues of faith, hope, and charity that are peculiar to Christianity and beyond the ken of pagan morality. They are the conditions for enjoying the beatific vision. Of course, the tendency to read the doctrinal cantos as a series of objective presentations is prompted by Dante's own words: "Just as the bachelor candidate must arm himself and does not speak until the master asks the question for discussion—for approval, not to conclude it—so while she spoke I armed myself with all my arguments, preparing for such a questioner and such professing" (*Par.* 24.46–51). And the first question put to him by St. Peter is, What is faith? No doubt there is an initial similarity to a scholarly examination, but that should not obscure the truly remarkable personal profession of this "candidate." Imagine him speaking thus in an ordinary academic oral exam—the difference leaps out at us.

Earlier, Peter had been identified as keeper of the keys, the head of the Church, but here, reference is made to his response to Jesus when he got out of the boat and tried to walk on water (Matt. 14:28–31). That is, Peter here is not the glorified saint but the Peter whose faith faltered as he walked upon the water, causing him to sink, and the Peter who denied Christ. Here, Peter is addressing a Dante who is still in the condition that the saint was on earth.

The examination began with the question, What is faith? Dante proceeds to quote St. Paul from Hebrews: "Faith is the substance of things hoped for, the evidence of things unseen."[4] That, Dante says in perfect Scholastic mode, is the quiddity of faith. "Why substance?" Peter then asks, and "Why evidence?" Dante's reply to the first is, "The profound things that bestow their image on me here are hidden from sight below, so that what they are lies in faith alone, and the highest hope is based on that faith; and so it is that faith is called a substance" (*Par.* 24.70–74). And what of "evidence"?

> E da questa credenza ci convene
> silogizzar, sanz' avere altra vista:
> però intenza d'argomento tene.
> *(Par.* 24.75–78)

From this faith it is meet that we begin to reason, although seeing no more; so faith is called an evidence.

So far, we seem indeed to be listening to a degree candidate being examined in a purely academic way. That what Dante is engaged in here is more a *confession* of faith than an *account* of it, however, is clear when we look at a thoroughly magisterial treatment of the subject, such as that of Thomas Aquinas.

In his commentary on Hebrews 11:1, "Faith is the substance of things to be hoped for, the existence of things that are not seen," Thomas states that this definition of faith is complete but obscure.[5] In the *Disputed Questions on Truth (De ver.)*, q. 14, a. 2, he puts it this way: This expression is the most perfect and complete definition of faith, but it is not expressed in the proper form of a definition. The proper form is to give the genus into which the nature of the thing in question fits, and its specific difference from other generically similar things. But, Thomas adds, it is easy to put this definition into the usual proper form—and that is what he goes about doing. Everything that is needed for a formal definition is provided in Paul's remark. There are three indications that this is so.

First, all the principles on which the essence of faith depends are given in the statement from Hebrews. Earlier, Thomas had stressed the crucial role of will in the act of faith; but will is moved by its object, which is the known desirable good, the end. For faith, two things are needed: the good moving the will; and that to which the intellect assents.

"There is a twofold ultimate good of man which first moves the will as its ultimate end" (*De ver.*, q. 14, a. 2).[6] Two ultimate goods act as our ultimate end. One is proportioned to our nature and can be attained by natural efforts, namely, the happiness of which philosophers speak, whether contemplative or practical. The other is a good that exceeds human nature, for the attaining of which natural powers are insufficient. But we cannot be ordered to an end unless there is in us some proportion to that end; that is, the loved is always similar to the lover.

With respect to the first ultimate good, we have a certain inchoative grasp of it, namely, in the first self-evident principles that are the seeds of theoretical and practical reasoning, as well as a natural desire for this good. There must be something analogous in the case of the ultimate good that exceeds our nature. The ultimate happiness, according to the philosophers, consists in such knowledge of God as we can attain by our natural powers. This is knowledge of God from His effects. But in the supernatural order we are called to a complete knowledge of God: "This is eternal life, that they might know thee, the one true God" (John 17:3). Faith is the name of that beginning in us of the complete knowledge of God. But in anything that has parts, the most fundamental part, the beginning of the whole, is called its substance. Thus faith, insofar as it is the beginning of eternal life, which we hope for on the basis of the divine promise, is called "the substance of things hoped for."

The assent of intellect to what is proposed to it—here, the articles of faith—is dependent on a movement of will, because the object in this case is not obviously true. In the usual case of assent, the mind grasps what is clear to it, proportioned to its natural powers, and goes on to argue from that truth to other truths. Similarly, the obscure things assented to in the act of faith are the basis on which arguments are formed. Hence, faith is the "argument for things which do not appear."

Thomas sums up: we are given the matter or object of faith, which is unseen (*non apparentium*); its act, in that it is an argument (*argumentum*); and the order to the end, in that it is the substance of things hoped for (*substantia rerum sperandarum*). The genus is given by its act, namely, a habit that is known from its act, and by its subject, mind—and that suffices. "Thus from what we are given it is easy to construct a well-formed definition of it; 'faith is a habit of mind by which eternal life begins in us and which causes the intellect to assent to what is not obvious'" *(De ver.* q. 14, a. 2*)*.

In his commentary on Hebrews, Thomas compares intellectual assent in natural learning with the assent of faith.[7] It is true that the mind normally assents to something because it *sees* it is so, and the process of arriving at this assent begins with a desire to know what a discipline promises. Any student must begin with a desire to know what is promised by the discipline and of which, of course, he or she is still ignorant. What is promised is thus seen as a good, something desirable, and the student's desire drives the intellect toward the acquisition of knowledge. Hence the adage, *oportet addiscentem credere*: the learner must believe. But the belief invoked in this example is human faith, that is, our trust in the teacher, and it is the start of a process that should end in our knowing on our own.[8] But although this likens divine faith to the trust and hope that is involved in any intellectual inquiry, the difference between the two is vast. Supernatural faith lasts as long as life does; it is only beyond our earthly life that the promised full knowledge will be obtained. Meanwhile, we see as in a glass darkly. In his commentary on Hebrews, just as in the *Disputed Questions on Truth*, Thomas also points out that divine faith differs from every other kind of mental act—from scientific knowledge, human faith, opinion, doubt, and conjecture.[9]

Once Peter has been assured that Dante can provide the quiddity, or the definition, of faith and can explain what enters into that definition, the exchange alters profoundly. "Do you have it in your purse?" Peter asks. That is to say, All right, you know what faith is, you have just explained it, but do you have it? The exchange may have continued for a time before being kicked into a first-person confessional form, but we sense that Peter and Dante are not discussing some interesting abstraction. Faith comes from the word of God and from miracles attesting to its veracity.

St. Peter declares himself satisfied with Dante's answers, "but now you must declare what you believe and what gave you the faith that you receive." And so we come to Dante's credo:

> E io rispondo: Io credo in uno Dio
> solo ed etterno, che tutto 'l ciel move,
> non moto, con amore e con disio;
> e a tal creder non ho io pur prove

fisice e metafisice, ma dalmi
anche la verità che quinci piove
    per Moïsè, per profeti e per salmi,
per l'Evangelio e per voi che scriveste
poi che l'ardente Spirto vi fé almi;
    e credo in tre persone etterne, e queste
credo una essenza sì una e sì trina,
che soffera congiunto 'sono' ed 'este.'
    De la profonda condizion divina
ch'io tocco mo, la mente mi sigilla
più volte l'evangelica dottrina.

    I answer: I believe in one God—sole,
eternal—He who, motionless, moves all
the heavens with His love and His desire;
    for this belief I have not only proofs
both physical and metaphysical;
I also have the truth that here rains down
    through Moses and the Prophets and the Psalms
and through the Gospels and through you who wrote
words given to you by the Holy Ghost.
    And I believe in three Eternal Persons,
and these I do believe to be one essence,
so single and threefold as to allow
    both *is* and *are*. Of this profound condition
of God that I have touched on, Gospel teaching
has often set the imprint on my mind.
                    (*Par.* 24.130–144, trans. Mandelbaum)

The first five lines express Dante's belief in God as the Prime Mover, about which doctrine he says he has physical and metaphysical proofs; then comes the assurance of Scripture. Personal as this testimony is, it also attests to Dante's months of study in Florence, as he prepared himself for his great task.

The truths about God that can be discovered by natural reason— that He exists, that He is one, that He is cause of all else, and the like—are of course implicit in the articles of the Nicene Creed. But the "preambles of faith" are not articles of faith and therefore do not as such enter into the creed.[10] Dante's profession of belief in the Trinity of Persons in God takes slightly over three lines, but this belief, unlike belief in God, rests entirely on the teaching of the Gospels.

Dante's creed, when compared to the Athanasian Creed, to the Apostle's Creed, or to the Nicene Creed, is pretty minimalist. There is a God, who is a Trinity of Persons. No mention is made of the things hoped for, of the Virgin Birth, or of the passion and death of Christ. Of course, Dante's credo here does not exhaust his faith—no creed is exhaustive—but what he professes here can be supplemented from the poem as a whole.

Uno attender certo de la gloria futura: A sure expectation of future glory

No doubt it is fitting that a canto dedicated to the virtue of hope (canto 25) should begin with Dante's wistful dream of returning to Florence, ending his long exile from his native city, and being granted the laurel crown for his sacred poem in the baptistry where his life of faith began. St. Peter himself has garlanded Dante's brow after his confession of faith. Of course, Florence did not follow suit. The sacred poem is drawing to its end—there are only a few cantos to go—but Dante will continue to eat the bread of others and climb the stairs of houses not his own.

> Se mai continga che 'l poema sacro
> al quale ha posto mano e cielo e terra,
> sì che m'ha fatto per molto anni macro,
>   vinca la crudeltà che fuor mi serra
> del bello ovile ov' io dormi' agnello,
> nimico ai lupi che li danno guerra;
>   con altra voce omai, con altro vello
> ritornerò poeta, e in sul fonte
> del mio battesmo prenderò 'l cappello;
>   però che ne la fede, che fa conte
> l'anime a Dio, quivi intra' io, e poi
> Pietro per lei sì mi girò la fronte.
>   (*Par.* 25.1–12)

Should this sacred poem, to which both heaven and earth have lent
a hand and which over the years has left me lean, ever overcome the
cruelty that keeps me from that fair fold in which as a lamb I slept,
a lamb opposed by wolves that war on it, then with other voice and
other fleece shall I return and at my baptismal font put on the laurel
crown; there I first found entry to the faith that reconciles souls with
God and for which Peter wreathed my brow.

After this melancholy prelude, the canto takes on its special meaning with the arrrival of a flame, circling like a dove and then alighting.
This is the soul of St. James, identified by reference to his burial place
in Compostela, a major object of pilgrimage in the Middle Ages and
now. As before, *modo academico*, Dante is asked by the apostle "to
tell what hope is, tell how it has blossomed within your mind" (*Par.*
25.46–47). Again, a duality: Dante must give an account of the virtue
itself and also how he personally acquired it. But before he can begin,
Beatrice intervenes, assuring St. James that there is "no child of the
Church Militant who has more hope than he has" (*Par.* 25.52–53). That
said, she leaves to Dante the response to St. James's two questions:

> "Spene," diss' io, "è uno attendar certo
> de la gloria futura, il qual produce
> grazia divina e precedente merto."
> (*Par.* 25.67–69)

> I said, "Hope is a certain expectation of future glory, produced by
> grace and preceding merit."

In response to this, James declares that he still burns with love "for
the virtue that was mine until my martyrdom and departure from
the field" (*Par.* 25.82–83). The sources of Dante's hope are to be found
in Holy Writ, as he explains, whereupon the blessed cry out *"Sperent
in te,"* They hope in you. This verse from Psalm 9:11 has already been
cited by Dante in speaking of the sources of his hope, and now it is
echoed by the blessed.

Toward the end of the canto, St. John arrives on the scene, announced by Beatrice in a pithy tercet.

"Questi è colui che giacque sopra 'l petto
del nostro pellicano, e questi fue
di su la croce al grande officio eletto."
                    (*Par.* 25.112–114)

This is he who laid his head upon the breast of Christ our pelican
and, from the cross, was chosen for a grand task.

What is the *grande officio* assigned to John by Jesus on the Cross?
"Then when Jesus saw his mother and the disciple whom he loved
standing there, he said to his mother, 'Woman, behold thy son,' and
then he said to the disciple, 'Behold thy mother.' And from that moment on the disciple took her into his household" (John 19:26–27).
The care of the Blessed Virgin fell to John, and she was with him for
the rest of her life. Mary thus enters obliquely into the discussion.
There is more, however. John, noticing that Dante is peering at him as
if to get a better look, makes it clear that his own body has been consigned to earth and will remain there until the dead are raised. Dante
is here addressing a legend that John had been assumed both body
and soul into heaven. Not so, says the one who would know. There
are only two presently in heaven as both body and soul, and they are
Jesus and His Blessed Mother.

Con le due stole nel beato chiostro
son le due luci sole che saliro;
e questo apporterai nel mondo vostro.
                    (*Par.* 25.127–129)

Only two lights have risen to our blessed choir with two robes: tell
this to the world.

Dante thus affirms the assumption of Mary at a time when even St.
Thomas considered it at most a possibility. Eventually, in 1950, the
assumption of Mary was declared *de fide,* infallible dogma. The idea
that it was fitting for the body of this most faithful one not to undergo
corruption, much discussed before the declaration, thus became a
settled truth of Catholic belief.[11]

Of the three theological virtues, only the third, charity, remains. After this life there is no further need for faith—its enigmatic knowledge gives way to vision—or of hope, since what was hoped for is now had. Dante's condition is still mortal, so he must exhibit his possession of all three virtues before he can be taken up into the highest heaven, where he will be granted a brief and privileged glimpse of things to come.

Filosofici argomenti e autorità

When Dante is being examined by St. John on charity, he states that love is imprinted on him "by philosophic arguments and by authority," and St. John repeats the phrase with obvious approval. Earlier, responding to St. Peter on faith, Dante had pointed to a syllogism that shows that faith is true (*Par.* 24.94). And in his credo, Dante insists that for beliefs in the first five lines, consisting of truths about God as Prime Mover, "I have not only proofs both physical and metaphysical" but revelation as well. St. John sums up Dante's position thus:

> E io udi': "Per intelletto umano
> e per autoritadi a lui concorde
> d'i tuoi amori a Dio guarda il sovrano."
> (*Par.* 26.46–48)

> And I heard, "By means of the human intellect and authority in concord with it, the highest of your loves to God will go."

Such passages do not prepare us for Beatrice's diatribe against the reasoning of the schools, which we find in canto 29. In the previous canto she had compared the theologies of (Pseudo-)Denis the Areopagite and Gregory the Great on the angelic hierarchies, indicating that Denis had it right and that when Gregory arrived in paradise, he smiled at his own earthly error. But this is only to point out that sometimes reasoning turns out well and sometimes it doesn't. There is far more at issue in canto 29. The reasoning of the schools is characterized as confused and ambiguous. And worse.

Voi non andate giù per un sentiero
filosofando: tanto vi trasporta
l'amor de l'apparenza e 'l suo pensiero!
    E ancor questo qua sù si comporta
con men disdegno che quando è posposta
la divina Scrittura o quando è torta.
                              (*Par.* 29.85–90)

You do not follow a single path when you philosophize down
there—love of showing off and of your own thinking! Yet all that
ostentation is disdained less here than when Sacred Scripture is
distorted or subordinated.

The specific problem under consideration here is the number of
the angels, but the criticism does not seem limited to that particular
issue. And there is also Beatrice's disdainful reference to Dante's studies in Florence. What is Dante's teaching on the relationship between
faith and reason, between faith and the desire to understand? Is there
a division of opinion between him and Beatrice?

    In the case of the first part of his credo, Dante has been taken to
be referring to such proofs as the *quinque viae* of Thomas Aquinas,
the five ways of proving the existence of God from premises that express truths about the world around us, truths available to any human
person. This is, of course, an appeal to a theological work, the *Summa
theologiae.* The question arises, what effect does the theological setting have on the so-called natural reasoning? Thomas himself coined
a phrase to name truths about God that can be established by "physical and metaphysical" reasoning. He called them *praeambula fidei,*
preambles of faith. He never provides an exhaustive list of these preambles, most often settling for such a list as "God exists," "There is
only one God," and the like. Thomas found the proofs in Aristotle's
Physics (books 7 and 8) and *Metaphysics* (book 12) cogent and em-
ployed them in his *Summa.* But these, and all other truths about God,
Thomas Aquinas, as a believer, would have held long before he was
capable of formulating or assessing a philosophical proof of them. In
short, the truths about God that philosophers can and have proved
are included among the truths about God that have been revealed.

Before the believer knows (by way of a philosophical proof) that God exists, he or she believes it. By calling such truths preambles of faith, Thomas is comparing them to faith, a comparison that only a theologian, not an ancient philosopher, would make. Does this render the relationship between the known and believed hopelessly ambiguous?

When Thomas says that there are two kinds of truth about God, those that can be known to be such and those that in this life can only be believed, he speaks of both of them as what "we profess."[12] Dante is clearly influenced by Thomas's claim that there are philosophical proofs of some of the truths about God that have been revealed. If philosophers of old could prove such truths, so can philosophers of any time, believers or not. We might wonder what interest believers would have in finding proofs for things they already hold to be true. We might further wonder, if we are like Thomas Aquinas, why God would include within revelation certain truths about Himself that can be known separately, and thus need not be believed on the basis of faith.[13]

The fact is that holding truths on the basis of faith is not a natural mode of the human mind. When we trust one another for some truth, this may be a mere expedient. I take your word that Beijing is a foggy city, and then I go there and know this to be true. The preambles of faith are like that. But what about all the other truths that have been revealed and are believed and that cannot in this life be known? Those are the mysteries of faith, the articles of faith. Do we just acknowledge that we cannot comprehend and fall silent?

St. Anselm's maxim *fides quaerens intellectum*—faith seeking understanding—has often been taken as the charter for believers pondering the *mysteries* of faith. That effort is distinguished from philosophical efforts, since the latter issue in knowledge. But the mysteries of the faith—the Incarnation, the Trinity, the forgiveness of sins, and so on—however much we reflect on them, compare them to knowledge, and defend them against the charge of incoherence, nonetheless resist our efforts to comprehend them. So long as we are alive, the only basis for holding the mysteries to be true is because God has revealed them. They are something the Church teaches us. Unlike the theology of the philosophers, which is the culminating achievement of philosophy, the theology based on Sacred Scripture, on revelation, always remains in a sense a learned ignorance, a *docta ignorantia*.

No wonder, then, that Thomas welcomes the results of philosophical theology, which he dubs the preambles of faith. They suggest the following argument for the reasonableness of faith, that is, the reasonableness of accepting as true what we cannot in this life *know* to be true. If some of the truths that have been revealed—the preambles—can be known to be true, this suggests that the whole of revelation consists of intelligible truths, truths that will be understood and grasped as true in the next world.

But why would the preambles be revealed? If they are knowable by our own efforts, why not simply trust people to learn them through natural reasoning and then go on to relate them to the mysteries of the faith? Despite his robust confidence in the range of reason, and despite his obvious admiration of Aristotle for having come to such knowledge of God as he could derive from his knowledge of the world, Thomas nonetheless holds that the human race would be in real trouble if those naturally knowable truths about God were not immediately available to all through revelation.[14] The theology of the philosophers is a difficult achievement; metaphysical proofs of God's existence, however cogent, are subject to endless discussion.

Dante's expression of confidence in the range of reason matches that of Thomas Aquinas. He is certainly not suggesting that the mysteries of faith can be established by philosophical argumentation, and his suggestion that even the truths that can be established by reason are corroborated by revelation is consistent with Thomas's view. This little dispute, to the degree that it is one, calls attention to a premise essential to Dante and the *Commedia*, namely, the compatibility of the natural and the supernatural and the complementarity of the best of reason and the mysteries of the faith.

Maior ex his est caritas: The greatest of these is love

The three theological virtues have God for their object, the God in whom one believes, the God for whom one hopes, and the God with whom one is eternally united in love. "There remain then these three, faith, hope, and charity, and the greatest of these is charity." With these words the magnificent chapter 13 of the First Epistle to the Corinthians ends. This being so, we might expect that St. John's examination of Dante on charity would be the most thorough of all. Actually, it is the briefest. St. John makes his appearance in canto 25, where his brilliance blinds Dante, a condition in which Dante remains until the examination is over.

In his response to John, Dante gives credit to Beatrice for awakening love in him (*Par.* 26.15). The alpha and omega of sacred writings, he continues, links love and the good.

> E io: "Per filosofici argomenti
> e per autorità che quinci scende
> cotale amor convien che in me si imprenti:
>   ché 'l bene, in quanto ben, come s'intende,
> così accende amore, e tanto maggio
> quanto più di bontate in sé comprende."
>   (*Par.* 26.25–30)

> And I answered, "By means of philosophical arguments and by the authority that descends from here, that love was impressed upon me. For the good as such, once understood, thus enkindles love, and all the more the more goodness in itself is understood."

We have already considered this blend of philosophical and authoritative (i.e., scriptural) bases for Dante's conception of the primacy of love. The cosmos is an ordered whole, and each thing in it naturally seeks its good. A thing can be directed to a good only if knowledge of that good is had, and for most things in the cosmos the knowledge involved in their natural appetites is not their own but their maker's. They fly to their assigned ends like an arrow to the target. Other cosmic entities have sense knowledge, and this is antecedent to their pursuit of pleasures and pains, the two being signs as to whether the thing sought is good or bad for the seeker. With humans a whole new realm opens up, involving intelligence and thus the capacity to grasp goodness as such and to direct ourselves to our true good.

We pointed out earlier that we are rational animals; that is, we have bodies and share many appetites and drives with brute animals; for that matter, we share properties with plants and even inanimate nature. We also have drives and appetites that follow more or less automatically on sense perception. But the human task is not to put one's mind to the more efficient or satisfying attainment of food and drink and sexual pleasure. These undeniable goods are parts of the human good insofar as they are ordered by and amenable to rational direction to one's overall good. The understood good, the object of intelligence, triggers that appetite we call will. Will is a natural appetite, to the extent that we cannot *not* will the good. Our task is to order other goods to that end, and here we may succeed or fail. Our animal appetites are at war with our pursuit of the rationally recognized good.

We naturally and necessarily want our comprehensive good, the end that is ultimate because, once obtained, there is nothing further to desire. In that sense, we can say that there is one single end for all human agents. But the drama arises from the fact that we identify that ultimate end with objects that can scarcely fulfill our expectations. Pleasure, wealth, power, fame—these and other objects have been put forward as identical with our ultimate end. If this were merely an intellectual problem, a misidentification that can be dealt with by argument, life would be simpler. As it is, we reveal our identification of lesser and evanescent goods and the ultimate end in our actions far more than in our theories. And in action, our emotions and passions are involved; we become habituated to seek, say, sense pleasure. It takes more than a convincing argument if we are to change our ways. It involves a struggle, the schooling of our sense appetite to respond to the true good. This is a struggle in which we need the help of friends, the support of the community in which we live, and, above all, God's grace.

No one becomes good by studying philosophy, Aristotle wrote. He meant that pondering about the good at a level of abstraction can never as such alter the condition of our appetite. The good that we would, we do not, and the good that we would not, we pursue. The paradox of human action is contained in this maxim. It is possible for weak persons to recognize their true good and yet not have the strength to overcome their habitual pursuit of something at odds with their true good.

Dante by contrast seems rather sanguine about the power of knowledge:

Dunque a l'essenza ov' è tanta avvantaggio,
che ciascun ben che fuor di lei si trova
altro non è ch'un lume di suo raggio,
    più che in altra convien che si mova
la mente, amando, di ciascun che cerne
il vero in che si fonda questa prova.
(Par. 26.31–36)

Hence to that Essence where there is such eminence that any other
good is merely a share of its light, any mind must be moved by love—
any mind that grasps the truth on which this proof is founded.

The good that engages the will initially and necessarily is the vague
conception of what will wholly fulfill desire. On reflection, we might
say with Aristotle that our good will be the perfection (virtue) of
our distinctive activity, which is rational activity. But as pointed out
in chapter 2, rational activity is not a single thing—sometimes the
phrase means the activity of reason as such, theoretical or practical,
and sometimes it means activities other than reasoning which are
directed by reason. There is a plurality of virtues perfecting each of
these kinds of rational activity, a plurality of intellectual virtues and a
plurality of moral virtues. From a purely philosophical point of view,
one might say not only that the moral virtues have their specific objects, but that their acquisition removes obstacles to the perfection of
mind as such, and the ultimate perfection of mind is the contemplation of eternal, divine things.

As we have discussed in earlier chapters, the ultimate end as understood by the Christian, and thus by Dante, is much, much more
than this. We are called to eternal union with God in love. This is
not something even dreamt of by philosophers. The philosophers of
course know of our warring appetites—how could they not? —but as
to why we are so divided against ourselves, they cannot say. The division is there, it constitutes our moral task, and that is enough. But if
in reality human beings are called to an end that philosophers could
not know, it would seem that philosophers cannot provide us with
useful guidance for our lives.

One must be careful here. St. Augustine once said that the virtues of the philosophers are in reality vices. And certainly they would be vices, if we thought that virtues as the philosophers talk of them, virtues that we can with however strenuous an effort acquire, are the means of achieving what we now know is our true end, our beatific union with God. Nonetheless, the philosopher can achieve a true if imperfect identification of our ultimate end. The morality that we find in Plato and Aristotle may not be the whole story, but surely we would not dismiss what they say of justice and courage and temperance as wholly false. What Thomas Aquinas suggests is that we must distinguish between an imperfect, inadequate understanding of our end and a perfect understanding of it. The latter is what we accept on the basis of faith. The natural and supernatural orders are thus distinct but related; the one cannot do service for the other.

A question that theologians have asked over the years, among them Thomas Aquinas, is whether we have a natural desire for the supernatural end. If the beatific vision is indeed the end to which men are called, their desire for it might be thought of either as a gift along with the object desired—thus a supernatural desire for a supernatural end—or as a natural desire. Why would anyone want to say that we have a natural desire for our supernatural end? Well, for one thing, the supernatural end is presented to us as the sum of all our desires. As Thomas noted, this amounts to the identification of our ultimate end with the beatific vision. But we desired our ultimate end before we knew it consisted in the beatific vision. What we naturally desire is whatever truly plays the role of our ultimate end. In that sense, we can be said naturally to desire the supernatural end.

But a supernatural end is by definition beyond our natural reach. Only with the aid of grace can we be turned toward our true end, toward God, through the theological virtues of faith, hope, and charity. St. Paul, referring to the altar of the Unknown God in Athens, could say that he has come to tell the Athenians of that God. So too, the preaching of the Good News is that this is our heart's desire. In Augustine's words, once again, "You have made us for yourself, O God, and our hearts are restless until they rest in thee." There is a continuity between the natural and supernatural, but it is an odd continuity, since one can achieve the supernatural only with the aid of grace. This is why Thomas calls the natural desire for a supernatural end an "obediential potency." We have the capacity for the supernatural, but we do not have the wherewithal to achieve it. Only with the help of grace can our natural desire for an all-fulfilling good be raised to faith that this good is to be found in the beatific vision.

St. John, as we saw above, declared: "By means of the human intellect and authority in concord with it, the highest of your loves to God will go." Is that all? Dante's reply to this is moving.

> Però ricominciai: "Tutti quei morsi
> che posson far lo cor volgere a Dio,
> a la mia caritate son concorsi:
>   ché l'essere del mondo e l'esser mio,
> la morte ch'el sostenne perch' io viva,
> e quel che spera ogne fedel com' io,
>   con la predetta conoscenza viva,
> tratto m'hanno del mar de l'amor torto,
> e del diritto m'han posto a la riva.
> (*Par.* 26.55–63)

So I began again. "My charity comes from all those things that turn the heart to God: the existence of the world and my own, the death that He suffered that I might live; that which is the hope of all believers and my own, along with the lived knowledge that I mentioned, have drawn me from a distorted love and put me onto the right path."

Di servo tratto a libertate: Brought from slavery to freedom

Beatrice, as we know, has been Dante's guide since their reunion in the Garden of Eden atop Mount Purgatory. Her scolding of him there served as a reminder of what underlies Dante's pilgrimage. He had fallen into mortal sin, his salvation was jeopardized by his actions, he found himself in a dark wood, lost, bewildered. We can all too easily get ourselves into such a predicament, but getting out is beyond our powers. The Mother of Mercy, painfully aware of Dante's plight, tells St. Lucy to speak to Beatrice about it. The importance of this sequence cannot be overstated. One's beloved may forget, a saint who has been the object of one's special devotion may need reminding, but the Blessed Virgin Mary is, so to speak, the sleepless refuge of sinners. She answers prayers even before they have been made. Dante has reminded us that he began and ended each day with a prayer to Mary. Mary is the prime mover of the *Commedia*. Yet we also must not overlook the significance of all the intermediate causes in the chain. Bestirred by St. Lucy, Beatrice goes to work to save the man who loves her. She leaves her position in heaven, her location in the celestial rose, and goes down into hell, where, in Limbo, she enlists the aid of Virgil, who will lead Dante until he reaches the summit of Mount Purgatory and Beatrice can take over.

By now, Beatrice has guided Dante up through the celestial spheres, and in the heaven of the fixed stars he has witnessed the triumph of Jesus and Mary as they ascend into the ultimate heaven, the tenth, the celestial empyrean, where all reference to visible corporeal things is absent. Before Dante can be taken higher, he is subjected to examination on the theological virtues by saints Peter, James, and John, respectively. Only then can Beatrice take him up into the realm of the angels. Beyond is the celestial empyrean. Dante gazes on the scene before him, the blessed forming a rose-like company. At this point, Beatrice leaves him, returning to her appointed place in the rose, and Dante's last guide takes over. He is St. Bernard of Clairvaux. His task is to obtain permission for Dante to glimpse, while still in his mortal body, God Himself, to have a foretaste of the beatific vision.

Consider the contrast with the beginning of the poem. Dante's plight was so bad that only the shock treatment of seeing the souls in hell seemed likely to bring about a change of heart. The beginning of wisdom is fear of the Lord. Masters of religious retreats once set the scene by preaching on the Four Last Things: Death, Judgment, Hell, and Heaven. St. Francis de Sales does much the same thing in his *Introduction to a Devout Life*. James Joyce provides a powerful sample of such sermons in his *Portrait of the Artist as a Young Man*. Anyone who finds such an approach a demeaning use of scare tactics, a Jesuitical trick to get the simple faithful firmly under the clerical thumb, will have trouble appreciating the opening cantica of the *Commedia*. The description of the Inferno is Dante's own, his imaginative and poetic achievement, but hell for him is not a fiction. The little seers of Fatima were given a glimpse of hell that lasted seconds and yet stirred them to their depths. The great alternatives, heaven or hell, underwrite the seriousness of the actions we perform. It matters how we act. Every agent knows that. Every act is a conscious choice of a course to which there is an alternative, and we are answerable for the choices we make. We become our choices, so to speak. Our character is built up of them, and every future choice reinforces or weakens that character. Only if it did not, finally, really matter what we do could the question of ultimate answerability be set aside. We should keep in mind the allegorical meaning of the *Commedia* as Dante stated it in his letter to Can Grande della Scala. The poem puts before us the way in which human beings, by the use of their free will, determine their just eternal condition.

Dante has come a long way since he found himself in that dark wood. The lesson of hell and of eternal punishment had been taught him as he descended deeper and deeper into the realm peopled by those who failed to fulfill the very purpose of their lives, their reason for being. It is the realm of despair. We detect a growing awareness in Dante of what he has done, of the fate he has been risking. In the second cantica he scales Mount Purgatory, as a penitent among penitents. By the time of his reunion with Beatrice, all of the *P*'s representing the capital sins have been erased from his forehead, indicating that recompense for them has been made. His sins have been forgiven, and he has been purged of their lingering taint. The waters of Lethe will wash away the very memory of those sins, and the waters of Eunoe will prepare him for what lies ahead.

When he ascends into the celestial empyrean, Dante attempts to describe what he is seeing. Describing his own feelings is easier. Imagine a barbarian's reaction on first seeing imperial Rome, and we will have some inkling of Dante's response on seeing heaven.

> ïo, che al divino da l'umano,
> a l'etterno dal tempo era venuto,

e di Fiorenza in popol giusto e sano,
   di che stupor dovea esser compiuto!
               (*Par.* 31.37–40)

What a stupor I was in when I came to the divine from the human,
to the eternal from time, to a people just and sane from Florence!

Consciousness of his own sinfulness never dims Dante's condemnation of political and ecclesiastical misbehavior. Thomas Aquinas, a Dominican, can praise Francis of Assisi, and Bonaventure, a Franciscan, can praise Dominic, but both lament the decadence in their own religious orders, each not yet a century old. So too, St. Benedict will recount with sadness the laxness that has crept into the monastic life. The view from above provides a very somber picture of mankind. Beatrice, in turn, will decry the follies of men. Only by allowing oneself to be led out of the dark wood will remedies for these moral evils come.

St. Bernard is Dante's final guide. Why Bernard?[15] Because of his profound devotion to Mary.

E la regina del cielo, ond' ïo ardo
tutto d'amor, ne farà ogne grazia,
però ch'i' sono il suo fedel Bernardo.
               (*Par.* 31.100–102)

The Queen of Heaven, for whom I wholly burn with love, will grant us every grace, since I am her faithful Bernard.

Before Bernard takes over, however, but after Beatrice returns to her place in the celestial rose, Dante makes a moving and impassioned declaration of his debt to her. This can be read as the apotheosis of what we already discerned in the *Vita Nuova*. The literal love of a young man for a beautiful woman is allegorically transformed into the story of his salvation.[16]

"O donna in cui la mia speranza vige,
e che soffristi per la mia salute
in inferno lasciar le tue vestige,

di tanti cose quant' i' ho vedute,
dal tuo podere e da la tua bontate
riconosco la grazia e la virtute.
   Tu m'hai di servo tratto a libertate
per tutte quelle vie, per tutt' i modi
che di ciò fare avei la potestate.
   La tua magnificenza in me custodi,
sì che l'anima mia, che fatt' hai sana,
piacente a te dal corpo si disnodi."
                                          (*Par.* 31.79–90)

O Lady, in whom my hope is strengthened and who for my
salvation's sake went down to Hell and left your footprints there, in
all that I have seen I realize the grace and virtue of your power and
goodness. You have drawn me from slavery to freedom by all the
paths and ways that are in your power to do so. May your generosity
keep my soul healthy so that you will find it pleasing when, freed
from the body, it comes to you.

We were struck in reading the *Vita Nuova* by the way in which
Beatrice seems to be a figure for the Blessed Virgin, so much so that
she sometimes takes on traits and privileges of Mary. Now, in the
Paradiso, this no longer surprises. Mary is the pattern of all virtues,
as we have learned in the *Purgatorio*. She who is full of grace will
function as a model for those whose grace is less but, as we shall see,
has been dispensed through Mary's hands. Now, in order for Dante
to be granted a glimpse of God, the intercession of Mary is required,
and Bernard has the credentials to address her. Mary is the queen to
whom this realm is subject and devoted (*Par.* 31.117). At Bernard's
urging, Dante lifts his eyes to look at Mary. He can only describe her
for us by indirection. Mary is looking at the angels swirling and singing around her.

Vidi a lor giochi quivi e a lor canti
ridere una bellezza, che letizia
era ne li occhi a tutti li altri santi.
                                          (*Par.* 31.133–135)

I saw then a Loveliness smiling at their play and song so that there was delight in the eyes of the other saints.

Mary is a mother smiling at her children at play. Her love is a maternal tenderness rather than the aloofness that the title Queen of Heaven might lead us to expect. Dante has seen Mary triumphant earlier, when she ascended into the empyrean with Her Son, but with this glimpse we enter the final phase of the sacred poem. From now on it is overtly dominated by the Blessed Virgin. The canto ends with Dante's description of the love with which Bernard looks to Mary.

The Face Most Like the Face of Christ

In the final two cantos of the *Paradiso*, Dante attempts to describe a world beyond the visible and to convey to us experiences so surpassing earthly ones that his task seems impossible, as indeed he himself says again and again. St. Paul has told us that eye has not seen nor ear heard nor has it entered into the heart of man to know what God has prepared for those who love Him. Yet Dante makes the attempt, and he succeeds because of the centrality of Mary, Queen of Heaven and Queen of the Angels. Her ultimate celestial role, taken by itself, may seem to heighten the problem that Dante faces—until he writes one of the most delightful tercets of the entire poem.

> Riguarda omai ne la faccia che a Cristo
> più si somiglia, ché la sua chiarezza
> sola ti può disporre a veder Cristo.
> (*Par.* 32.85–87)

Look now on that face that most resembles that of Christ; its brightness alone can dispose you to see Christ.

This is a recurrent theme in Bernard's sermons and other writings: Mary is the path by which we go to Christ, just as she was the means of His coming among us as the Incarnate God. In order to fulfill this providential role, Mary was accorded graces beyond measure—*gratia plena*—more than any other mere human being, and more than any angel. In this realm of unimaginable bliss, where images and metaphors are of little help, we suddenly have the reminder that Mary, the Lady of Heaven on her throne of glory (*Par.* 32.29–30), is also the young woman who gave birth to Jesus in a Bethlehem stable. His mother! Of course the son will resemble the mother, and vice versa; what else does family resemblance mean? The virgin whose Fiat complements the Fiat of creation accepts the angel's message and opens the way to salvation.

> La piaga che Maria richiuse e unse,
> quella ch'è tanto bella da' suoi piedi
> è colei che l'aperse e che la punse.
>
> (*Par.* 32.4–6)

The wound that Mary healed and medicated, is that which Eve, now sitting all lovely at her feet, pierced open.

The uniqueness of Mary's role in the providential plan explains her place in the celestial empyrean and the love and devotion shown to her by the blessed. If Mary had not accepted the angel's message, none of them would be here.[17] Their salvation literally hung on her agreement, since without it there would have been no God Man whose sacrifice and death opened the gates of heaven. Other advocates we may have, other guides whose prompting and invocations help us on our way. But none of them approaches the primacy of Mary in this regard. In giving birth to the God Man, she becomes an integral part of the redemptive plan. She is full of grace. That is meant as a superlative; no other creature approaches her in holiness or is more intimately bound up with the life of God. Mary is not only the Mother of the Savior, she is the mother of those He saves. Her role is not exhausted by the biological fact that she carried Jesus in her womb for nine months. But even that period of waiting involved a unique closeness of creature and God, an intimacy no other creature could have: flesh of her flesh, bone of her bone. In the Incarnation we see the fusing of the roles of natural mother and supernatural mother of those Jesus came to save.

Notice how Bernard moves easily from the reminder of the family resemblance between Mary and her son to the mediating role she plays. Look at her face, he urges Dante, the face so like the face of Christ, for "its brightness alone can dispose you to see Christ."[18] Mary is the way to Jesus, to the beatific vision. Dante has Bernard suggest that there is no way anyone can bypass her and still come to God.

Earlier, an angel had been observed hovering over Mary. The angel now begins to sing "Ave Maria, gratia plena," Hail, Mary, full of grace, and the whole heavenly court takes up the salutation. The angel is Gabriel, the angel of the Annunciation. Bernard explains:

> Ed elli a me: "Baldezza e leggiadria
> quant' esser puote in angelo e in alma,
> tutta è in lui; e sì volem che sia,
>   perch' elli è quelli che portò la palma
> giuso a Maria, quando 'l Figliuol di Dio
> carcar si volse de la nosta salma."
>   (*Par.* 32.109–114)

> He said to me, "Whatever of gallantry and elegance can exist in any angel or soul is all in him, and rightly so in him who carried the palm to Mary below, when the Son of God took on the burden of our flesh."

As if to underscore the human, flesh-and-blood relationship of mother and son, Bernard points out Anna, Mary's mother, "so pleased to see her daughter that, as Anna sings hosanna, she does not move her eyes" (*Par.* 32.134–135). Anna is the grandmother of Jesus. Anna's presence brings home the marvel of the Incarnate God, who is like us in everything save sin.

The survey of the blessed, arrayed rose-like before Dante and Bernard, would not be complete without mention of St. Lucy, "she who urged on your lady when you bent your brows downward, to your ruin" (*Par.* 32.137–138). This is the final allusion to the long pilgrimage Dante has taken and how and under what auspices it began. His destination has been reached. He has arrived in the empyrean, the tenth heaven, the destined home of the blessed. And they are blessed because they see God. In that vision human happiness is complete. Only one thing remains, and that is for Dante to be given an experience not accorded to mortal men. Only by the intercession of Mary will this special grace be granted him—a taste of that beatifying vision. Earlier, Bernard had assured Dante that she "will grant us every grace" (*Par.* 31.101). Now, Bernard urges Dante to pray for the grace to penetrate the divine radiance "from that one who has the power to help you" (*Par.* 32.148). He is to do this by following along as Bernard prays. And thus the transition is made to the final canto.

Figlia del tuo figlio

The final canto of the *Paradiso*, as well as the final canto of the *Commedia*, begins with Bernard's magnificent prayer to the Blessed Virgin, in which he beseeches her to obtain for Dante the grace of a vision of God. That vision will be the culmination of Dante's pilgrimage. It is the completion of the long journey from his initial state of sinfulness, through the underworld of Hell, where the seriousness of human life and the imperative to live it well are brought home to him by seeing those whose sins have cut them off forever from their very reason for being—union with God. Like Dante, they preferred lesser goods to the greatest good, but unlike Dante and ourselves, all opportunity of conversion and change is gone for them. On then to Purgatory, where Dante joins the souls who are destined for beatitude but must first undergo a period of penance to purge their souls of the effects of their forgiven sins. Having reached the summit of Mount Purgatory, he is reunited with Beatrice at last, and she takes over from Virgil to lead him on to the next realm, the heavenly paradise which makes up immeasurably for that earthly one and where he will see what God has in store for those who love Him. Up through the gradations of blessedness, represented by the Ptolemaic planets, they emerge into the highest heaven, the celestial empyrean, where all the blessed actually dwell. The vast throng is presented to him in the form of a rose in which the blessed are arranged hierarchically. And he lifts his eyes to see Mary, the Queen of Heaven. Suddenly, Beatrice is no longer his guide; he finds himself with Bernard of Clairvaux, whose devotion to Mary was legendary. The only way Dante will be able to see, however briefly, God himself in the trinity of Persons is if Mary obtains for him the grace to do so. It is Bernard's task to beg her to bestow that grace. And so he begins his prayer.

> "Vergine Madre, figlia del tuo figlio,
> umile e alta più che creatura,
> termine fisso d'etterno consiglio,
>   tu se' colei che l'umana natura
> nobilitasti sì, che 'l suo fattore
> non disdegnò di farsi sua fattura.
>   Nel ventre tuo si raccese l'amore,
> per lo cui caldo ne l'etterna pace
> così è germinato questo fiore.
>   Qui se' a noi meridïana face
> di caritate, e giuso, intra ' mortali,
> se' di speranza fontana vivace.
>   Donna, se' tanto grande e tanto vali,
> che qual vuol grazia e a te non ricorre,
> sua disïanza vuol volar sanz' ali.
>   La tua benignità non pur soccorre
> a chi domanda, ma molte fiate
> liberamente al dimandar precorre.
>   In te misericordia, in te pietate,
> in te magnificenza, in te s'aduna
> quantunque in creatura è di bontate."
>
>   (*Par.* 33.1–21)

In Mandelbaum's translation of this canto,[19]

> "Virgin mother, daughter of your Son,
> more humble and sublime than any creature,
> fixed good decreed from all eternity,
>   you are the one who gave to human nature
> so much nobility that its Creator
> did not disdain His being made its creature.
>   That love whose warmth allowed this flower to bloom
> within the everlasting peace—was love

rekindled in your womb; for us above,
    you are the noonday torch of charity,
and there below, on earth, among the mortals,
you are a living spring of hope. Lady,
    you are so high, you can so intercede,
that he who would have grace but does not seek
your aid, may long to fly but has no wings.
    Your loving-kindness does not only answer
the one who asks, but it is often ready
to answer freely long before the asking.
    In you compassion is, in you is pity,
in you is generosity, in you
is every goodness found in any creature."

This first part of Bernard's prayer consists of praise of Mary and is a veritable florilegium of her titles and privileges. At once virgin and mother, the virginity of Mary before and after the birth of Christ is a firm part of traditional belief. Her son being divine, Mary paradoxically becomes the daughter of her son, but of course her daughtership and his sonship are quite different relations of dependence. That a mere creature could give birth to God, to be quite truly designated as the Mother of God, is a paradox captured often in the liturgy: "Genuisti qui te fecit" (You have given birth to the one who created you); "Quem caeli capere non poterant, tuo gremio contulisti" (He whom the heavens cannot contain was contained in your womb). It is this that places a humble young woman at the very apex of creation, as part of a plan from all eternity. By her conduct she has so ennobled the race that the creator did not disdain becoming her son. It was Mary's love, Bernard continues, that "allowed this flower to bloom," that is, the whole company of the blessed. No wonder their voices rise in praise and gratitude to Mary. "Ave Maria, gratia plena." She is the living torch of charity "above" and a living spring of hope for those "below." Once more, Dante reminds us that of the theological virtues, only charity remains in heaven; hope and faith mark the condition of the church militant. All this is by way of preparation for an extraordinary acknowledgment in Bernard's prayer of Mary's continuing providential role. Grace comes to us only through the hands of Mary: she is the mediatrix of grace. Any attempt to bypass her is like a wingless bird attempting flight. This is not a role conferred on Mary by the blessed or by those who intercede with her. God chose to come to us through Mary, and we are to go to him through Mary. As has been mentioned long before, in the *Purgatorio*, Mary is ready to give grace even before it is asked. She is the compassionate one, the one who has pity on us and is correspondingly generous. In Mary is "every goodness found in any creature." That is, Mary is the most perfect of God's creatures, thanks to the grace she has received that exceeds that of any other creature. She is placed above the choirs of angels, although from a natural point of view, the lowest angel is higher than the most talented human. But we are in the supernatural order—the divine plan formulated to redeem sinful mankind and calling us to a happiness far exceeding what Adam lost by his sin. We have seen the comparison of Eve and Mary: Eve is the mother of sinful mankind; Mary the mother of God and of all those God has chosen to save.

No one can fail to sense the devotion throbbing in these verses. Their spokesman is at once a historical figure—the saintly abbot of Clairvaux, advisor of popes, preacher of Crusades, foe of Abelard—and the author of sermons and commentaries exhibiting his profound devotion to Mary. It is these works that Dante knew and on which he bases the lines he attributes to Bernard in the *Paradiso*. Every utterance in this prayer can be matched with passages from Bernard himself. When we consider all of the great saints and theologians who have appeared during the upward flight of Dante and Beatrice, we find some, St. Bonaventure, certainly, whose fervor in writing of Mary matches that of Bernard. Nevertheless, Dante's selection of Bernard for this key role in the final canto both has historical grounding and doubtless reflects a personal preference as well. Bernard's prayer continues,

> "Or questi, che da l'infima lacuna
> de l'universo infin qui ha vedute
> le vite spiritali ad una ad una,
>
> supplica a te, per grazia, di virtute
> tanto, che possa con li occhi levarsi

più alto verso l'ultima salute.
    E io, che mai per mio veder non arsi
più ch'i' fo per lo suo, tutti miei prieghi
ti porgo, e priego che non sieno scarsi,
    perché tu ogne nube li disleghi
di sua mortalità co' prieghi tuoi,
sì che 'l sommo piacer li si dispieghi."
                    (*Par.* 33.22–33)

"This man—who from the deepest hollow in
the universe, up to this height, has seen
the lives of spirits, one by one—now pleads
    with you, through grace, to grant him so much virtue
that he may lift his vision higher still—
may lift it toward the ultimate salvation.
    And I, who never burned for my own vision
more than I burn for his, do offer you
all of my prayers—and pray that they may not
    fall short—that, with your prayers, you may disperse
all of the clouds of his mortality
so that the Highest Joy be his to see."

In this part of his prayer, Bernard makes his petition: let this mortal who has been led up from the depths of hell be permitted, mortal though he is, to see the One who is the alpha and omega of all things, the telos of creation, our reason for being, possession of whom, if granted by his grace, will more than fulfill every desire of the human heart. We notice Bernard's statement that he is as eager for Dante's vision as he ever was for his own. Doubtless this is the symmetrical counterpart of Dante's devotion to Bernard. Even so, it seems an extraordinary remark.[20] But Dante is surely not about to falter at this point in his continuing assumption that his own story, his own fate, and his own salvation possess cosmic importance. Now here he is, a mortal among the immortals, a welcome guest, waiting while one of the great mystics implores Mary to grant Dante a taste of the beatific vision. Is this hubris? Once more we have to consider the genesis of his pilgrimage: Mary summoned him and led him by means of intermediary guides to this point, where her faithful Bernard can ask Mary in effect to complete the pilgrimage she has instigated. We can never forget that the *Commedia* is the story of Dante's salvation, and that he is now spiritually prepared for what is about to happen, thanks to the pleas of Bernard and the compassion of Mary.

> "Ancor ti priego, regina, che puoi
> ciò che tu vuoli, che conservi sani,
> dopo tanto veder, li affetti suoi.
>
> Vinca tua guardia i movimenti umani:
> vedi Beatrice con quanti beati
> per li miei prieghi ti chiudon le mani!"
>
> (*Par.* 33.34–39)

> "This too, o Queen, who can do what you would,
> I ask of you: that after such a vision,
> his sentiments preserve their perseverance.
>
> May your protection curb his mortal passions.
> See Beatrice—how many saints with her!
> They join my prayers! They clasp their hands to you!"

The prayer ends here, with Bernard's hope that Dante, having been accorded a foretaste of eternity, will not lapse into the faults of old on returning to his still unfinished mortal life. This brings home yet again the central reminder of the poem. As long as we are alive we can repent and change our lives, or we can succumb to the passions and to sin. Call no man happy while he is yet alive, the ancients said (although they were thinking rather of one's posthumous reputation). Dante's point is that we can call no man definitively happy, or the reverse, until he is dead.

Lasciare alla futura gente: Leave for a future people

When Mary indicates her assent to Bernard's request, it is with a smile, with the expression of her eyes. Dante would never put words of his in her mouth. Things happen rapidly now. The poet has difficulty describing what he was permitted to see. Bernard signals what Dante is to do, but there is no need of that. Dante has already lifted his purified sight to the ray of Light. Light is the element of the empyrean, a supernatural, spiritual light, and the light at which Dante now gazes is God. Of course, words fail him. The narrative now becomes a recollection of the experience, rather than a present report of it.

> O somma luce che tanto ti levi
> da' concetti mortali, al a mia mente
> ripresta un poco di quel che parevi,
>   e fa la lingua mia tanto possente,
> ch'una favilla sol de la tua gloria
> possa lasciare a la futura gente;
>   ché, per tornare alquanto a mia memoria
> e per sonare un poco in questi versi,
> più si conceperà di tua vittoria.
>   (*Par.* 33.67–75)

> O Highest Light, You, raised so far above
> the minds of mortals, to my memory
> give back something of Your epiphany,
>   and make my tongue so powerful that I
> may leave to people of the future one
> gleam of the glory that is Yours, for by
>   returning somewhat to my memory
> and echoing awhile within these lines,
> Your victory will be more understood.

Continuing to look into the ray of light, he felt that he would have gone astray if he dared turn his eyes away. His vision reaches the Infinite Goodness.

> Oh abbondante grazia ond' io presunsi
> ficcar lo viso per la luce etterna,
> tanto che la veduta vi consunsi!
>   (*Par.* 33.82–84)

> O grace abounding, through which I presumed
> to set my eyes on the Eternal Light
> so long that I spent all my sight on it!

And what does he see? In the depths of that Light, that Infinite Goodness, he sees everything that is scattered and separate in the universe—substance and accidents, dispositions—all as if united. He has gone beyond beings to the Being that contains the sum of all perfections, perfections merely participated in by creatures. However unsatisfying his description of it, Dante feels a keen joy in making the effort. The moment of his vision outweighs twenty-five centuries. Caught up in a mystic rapture, his mind was "intent, steadfast, and motionless—gazing; and it grew ever more enkindled as it watched" (*Par.* 33.98–99).

> A quella luce cotal si diventa,
> che volgersi da lei per altro aspetto
> è impossibil che mai si consenta;
> però che 'l ben, ch'è del volere obietto,
> tutto s'accoglie in lei, e fuor di quella
> è defettivo ciò ch'è lì perfetto.
> (Par. 33.100–105)

> Whoever sees that Light is soon made such
> that it would be impossible for him
> to set that Light aside for other sight;
> because the good, the object of the will,
> is fully gathered in that Light; outside
> that Light, what there is perfect is defective.

The Light is Goodness itself, and all created goods, however perfect of their kind, are by comparison imperfect. All the longing of the human heart is satisfied here; Goodness contains all and more than one had sought in lesser goods.

Dante continues to gaze on the Light that is God, and as he does his vision goes deeper still. The Trinity of Persons in the godhead becomes, as it were, visible as interpenetrating circles of light within the Light, of different colors as they move.

> Ne la profonda e chiara sussistenza
> de l'alto lume parvermi tre giri
> di tre colori e d'una contenenza;
>   e l'un da l'altro come iri da iri
> parea reflesso, e 'l terzo parea foco
> che quinci e quindi igualmente si spiri.
>   (*Par.* 33.115–120)

>   In the deep and bright
>   essence of that exalted Light, three circles
> appeared to me; they had three different colors,
> but all of them were of the same dimension;
>   one circle seemed reflected by the second,
> as rainbow is by rainbow, and the third
> seemed fire breathed equally by those two circles.

Because we are listening to a remembered experience, a first-person narrative, we tend to forget that Dante Alighieri is attempting in human language to give expression to the ultimate mystery, the Trinity of Persons in the One God. Once more, he disarms us by exclaiming that his words are inadequate to the experience, but of course the experience is as artful as the words that express it. He is describing an imagined mystic experience. Poetic daring could scarcely go beyond this. Then Dante retreats to the comparative safety of theological expressions.

> O luce etterna che sola in te sidi,
> sola t'intendi, e da te intelletta
> e intendente te ami e arridi!
>   (*Par.* 33.124–126)

> Eternal Light, You only dwell within
> Yourself, and only You know You; Self-knowing,
> Self known, You love and smile upon Yourself!

Dante is describing Aristotle's concept of Thought Thinking Itself. Perhaps we sense relief in this appeal to another effort, a speculative effort, to express in human terms the nature of God. Does Dante also glimpse how we are made in the image of God? He wishes to know this, compares such an effort to squaring the circle, yet adds,

> se non che la mia mente fu percossa
> da un fulgore in che sua voglia venne.
> *(Par.* 33.140–141)

> But then my mind was struck by light that flashed
> and, with this light, received what it had asked.

Dante's vision is now over, but his desire and will are moved, like a rotating wheel, by "l'amor che move il sole e l'altre stelle"—"the Love that moves the sun and the other stars" *(Par.* 33.145).

EPILOGUE

The great French mathematician and philosopher Blaise Pascal had a mystical experience, a kind of private revelation, that changed his life. He wrote down a description in French and Latin and wore a copy next to his heart for the rest of his life. It is known as Pascal's Memorial:[1]

> Fire.
> God of Abraham, God of Isaac, God of Jacob,
> not of the philosophers and the learned.
> Certainty, certainty, feeling, joy, peace.
> *God of Jesus Christ,*
> My God and your God.
> Your God will be my God.
> The world and everything but God forgotten.
> He can be found only by the paths taught in the Gospel.
> The grandeur of the human soul.
> The Just Father whom the world has not known, but I have known Him.
> Joy, joy, joy, tears of joy.
> I have separated myself from him:
> They have forsaken me, the fount of living water.
> My God, do not abandon me
> Lest I be eternally separated from you.

This is eternal life, that they should know the one true God and the one
  whom He has sent, Jesus Christ.
Jesus Christ.
I have abandoned him, fled him, renounced and crucified him.
May I never be separated from him.
He can be had only by the paths taught in the Gospel.
Total and sweet renunciation. Etc.
Total submission to Jesus Christ and to my director.
Eternally in joy for a day of testing on earth.
May I not forget your words. Amen.

We notice the reference in the first line to fire to express the vision, perhaps similar to Dante's reliance on light in canto 33 of the
Paradiso. The message in these disconnected and fragmentary lines
may let us down, but we must remember that the Memorial was a
private note, addressed to himself. Pascal never intended it to be pub-
lished. Pascal was attempting to record what cannot engage the mind
or heart of just any passerby, any scholarly voyeur. Kierkegaard once
quoted a remark of Lichtenberg on Scripture: "Such works are like
mirrors. If a monkey looks in, no apostle looks out." Dante makes
similar demands.

Unlike Pascal in the Memorial, Dante was not writing for himself
alone. And we know who his intended readers were: all those who
by their free acts are justly earning an eternal reward or punishment.
Few readers can fail to respond to the exquisite art with which he has
put before us his imaginary pilgrimage—imaginary only in a sense.
Human life and its destiny provide the spine of this story, and Dante
was not making that up. Keen as our aesthetic enjoyment of the *Commedia* may be, intriguing as are the intellectual elements of the narrative, we know that Dante was after a deeper response than those. He
wanted to move us from the misery of sin to eternal happiness. And
he shows us the inescapable centrality of the Blessed Virgin Mary in
that conversion.

NOTES

Prologue

1. Hellmut Schnackenburg, *Maria in Dantes Göttlicher Komödie* (Freiburg in Breisgau: Herder, 1956); Jaroslav Pelikan, *Eternal Feminines: Three Theological Allegories in Dante's Paradiso* (New Brunswick, N.J.: Rutgers University Press, 1990); Domenico Bassi, *Il Mese di Maggio con Dante* (Rome: Opera Nazionale per il Mezzogiorno d'Italia, 1921); Renato Nicodemo, *La Vergine Maria nella Divina Commedia* (Florence: Firenze Atheneum, 2001). To these I add the perennial work of Frédéric Ozanam, *Dante and Catholic Philosophy in the Thirteenth Century*, trans. Lucia D. Pychowska (New York: The Cathedral Library Association, 1913).

2. See Louis-Marie Grignion de Montfort, *A Treatise on the True Devotion to the Blessed Virgin Mary* (Bay Shore, N.Y.: Montfort Fathers, 1941).

3. See, for example, De Koninck's "Pour nos frères dans le Christ," in *Tout homme est mon prochain* (Quebec: Les Presses de l'Université Laval, 1964), pp. 17ff. An English translation of this work will appear in a forthcoming volume of *The Writings of Charles De Koninck* (University of Notre Dame Press).

4. Charles DeKoninck, *Ego Sapientia: La sagesse qui est Marie* (Quebec: Fides, 1943). An English translation appears in volume 2 of *The Writings of Charles De Koninck*, ed. and trans. Ralph McInerny (Notre Dame, Ind.: University of Notre Dame Press, 2009).

5. In the essay by Jorge Louis Borges, "The Divine Comedy," included in *The Poets' Dante*, ed. Peter S. Hawkins and Rachel Jacoff (New York: Farrar, Straus and Giroux, 2001), p. 118.

6. Paul Claudel, "Introduction à un poème sur Dante," in *Oeuvres en prose*, Bibliothèque de la Pléiade (Paris: Gallimard, 1965), pp. 422ff.

ONE.   *A New Life Begins*

1. That Beatrice does not share this view is clear from *Purgatorio* 30 and 31, where she chides Dante for his fickleness.

2. Calling the great poem the *Divine Comedy* is established usage, even though Dante himself never referred to it in that way, but simply as the *Commedia*.

3. *Super Missus Est*, Homilia IV, 1; *Sancti Bernardi Opera Omnia*, ed. Mabillon (Paris, 1839), vol. 1, Tomus tertius, 1694.

4. *VN* 2. In Dante Alighieri, *Vita Nova*, a cura Luca Carlo Rossi, Introduzione Guglielmo Gorni (Milan: Arnoldo Mondadori, 1999). Hereafter, Rossi, *Vita Nova*.

5. Dante also introduced her as *la gloriosa donna* ("in glory," that is, in Paradise).

6. Dante Gabriel Rossetti, in *The Portable Dante*, ed. Paolo Milano (New York: Viking Penguin, 1969), pp. 550–51.

7. See for example, Rossi's commentary in *Vita Nova*, p. 13, on this passage. We are asked to think of Luke 3:16, and the words of John the Baptist: "I indeed baptize you with water, but there comes one stronger than I."

8. Beatrice died in 1290; Dante married Gemma in 1285.

9. See Charles Singleton, *An Essay on the Vita Nuova* (Baltimore: Johns Hopkins University Press, 1949), pp. 63–74.

10. Who has ever been truly surprised by Chaucer's Retractions, in which the maker of this book—*The Canterbury Tales*—takes his leave: "Wherefore I beseech you meekly for the mercy of God to pray for me, that Christ have mercy on me and forgive me my sins: and especially for my translations and inditings of worldly vanities, which I revoke in my retractions: as are the book of *Troilus*; also the book of *Fame*; the book of *The Nineteen Ladies;* the book of *The Duchess*; the book of *St Valentine's Day of the Parliament of Fowls*; *The Tales of Canterbury*, those that tend towards sin; the book of *The Lion*; and many another book, if they were in my memory; and many a song and many a lecherous lay; that Christ in his great mercy forgive me the sin." Chaucer, *The Canterbury Tales*, a new translation by Nevill Coghill (Baltimore: Penguin Classics, 1952), p. 513.

11. In his remarks prior to *VN* 19, Rossi, *Vita Nova*, p. 150, notes that only two persons have been raised body and soul into heaven, Christ and Mary. This is insisted on in the *Paradiso*, when St. John dismisses the legend that he too is in heaven body and soul.

12. Gorni, in his introduction to Rossi, *Vita Nova*, p. xvi.

13. Ibid., p. xviii.

14. Dante tells us that this training cost him thirty months attendance in the schools of the religious and at philosophical disputations. In so short a time he came to savor the sweetness of wisdom which drove out all else (*Convivio* 2.12).

TWO.   *In the Midst of My Days*

1. *The Divine Comedy*, trans. Dorothy L. Sayers, vol. 1, *Hell* (Hammersmith: Penguin Books, 1949), p. 71.

2. Guglielmo Gorni, one of the most helpful of Dante scholars, has dedicated an entire book to this opening canto of the *Comedy*. See Gorni, *Dante nella Selva, Il Primo canto della Commedia* (Parma: Pratiche Editrice, 1995).

3. Maurice Baring, in *Have You Anything To Declare?* (New York: Alfred A. Knopf, 1937), pp. 127–29, noting that it was under the influence of the German higher criticism of the Bible that Ernest Renan lost his faith, adds intriguingly that many, in following the course of Renan's argument, have been led into the faith the great apostate lost. Baring also suggests that if only Renan had lived to see what such criticism did to Shakespeare, he might himself have retraced his steps.

4. C. S. Lewis, *An Experiment in Criticism* (Cambridge: Cambridge University Press, 1961).

5. According to Robert Hollander on the letter and the controversies it has generated, this approach is reasonably well-grounded. See Robert Hollander, *Dante's Epistle to Cangrande* (Ann Arbor: University of Michigan Press, 1993).

6. *Convivio* 1.1. See also Jean Pépin, *Dante et la tradition de l'allégorie* (Montreal: Vrin, 1970).

7. Cicero, in his *De senectute* (On Old Age), a favorite of Dante's, discusses the *aetas media* in section 76. A current Italian translation of Cicero, facing the Latin text, renders this unbashedly as "si trova 'nel mezzo del cammin di nostra vita,'" that is, "finds himself 'Midway this way of life we're bound upon.'" Cicerone, *De senectute, De amicitia*, a cura Guerino Pacitti, Classici Greci e Latini 109 (Milan: Oscar Mondadori, 1965), p. 73.

8. Thomas's commentary on 2 Corinthians can be found in *Super Epistolas S. Pauli Lectura*, ed. Raphaelis Cai, O.P., editio 8 revisa, vol. 1 (Turin: Marietti, 1953).

9. The jingle runs,

> George Brush is my name;
> America's my nation;
> Ludington's my dwelling-place
> And heaven's my destination.

The proper name and home town, of course, varied with the pupil. See Thornton Wilder, *Heaven's My Destination* (New York: Harper & Brothers, 1935).

10. In a much later book, *The Eighth Day*, addressing a more jaded reader, Wilder ends his fascinating story thus: "History is *one* tapestry. No eye can venture to compass more than a hand's breadth. . . . There is much talk of a design in the arras. Some are certain they see it. Some see what they have been told to see. Some remember that they saw it once but have lost it, Some are strengthened by seeing a pattern wherein the oppressed and exploited of the earth are

gradually emerging from their bondage. Some find strength in the conviction that there is nothing to see. Some" Here the sentence and the book ends. One is tempted to complete it thus: Some, like Dante, with a vision infused with faith, give us the truth of the matter.

11. Thus begins the fifth of the "Divine Poems." John Donne, *Poetical Works*, ed. Herbert J. C. Grierson (Oxford: Oxford University Press, 1971), p. 295.

12. This *veltro,* or greyhound, who will come and solve the political problems of the age can serve as an indicator of the risks of scholarship. Since Virgil is making a prediction, it would seem fairly easy to identify this savior *ex post facto*. But perhaps more ink has been spilled on this single reference than on any other.

13. I am summarizing the opening five questions of *Summa theologiae* IaIIae (First Part of the Second Part), and *Nicomachean Ethics* 1.13 and St. Thomas's commentary thereon.

14. This seems strong, if Virgil was simply born at a time and place where the Good News could not have come to him. Elsewhere, Virgil stresses that he is in Limbo through no fault of his own.

THREE.   *The Seven Storey Mountain*

1. The second part of the angelic salutation, "Holy Mary," and so forth, was added in 431 by Pope St. Celestine I in response to the heresy of Nestorius. Paul Claudel, *Journal*, vol. 2 (Paris: Gallimard, 1969), p. 497.

2. Virtues and vices are habits, settled dispositions to act well or badly, but habits are built of singular acts, good or bad, and lead us on to others of the same kind. Whenever the "age of reason" begins—and who does not remember his first awareness of doing wrong?—from its dawn, we are forming by means of the ways we act what we morally are, that is, our character.

3. Boethius, *Consolation of Philosophy* 3.1.

4. Wallace Stevens, in section 11 of "Le Monocle de Mon Oncle."

5. Thomas, in *Super Evangelium S. Matthei Lectura*, ed. Raphaelis Cai, O.P., editio 5 revisa (Turin: Marietti, 1951), n. 400.

6. Ibid., n. 403.

7. Ibid., n. 404.

8. Although the treatment in the *Summa theologiae* is later than that of the *Disputed Questions on Evil* (*De malo*), I am guided chiefly by the latter. The plan of the *Summa* dictated that discussions of the capital sins are scattered; in the *De malo* we find a treatment of the capital sins as such, beginning with q. 8.

9. In an old academic joke, a professor dies and appears before St. Peter, who checks the records, shakes his head, and tells the professor he must go to hell. Immediately the professor finds himself in a well-appointed apartment; there are his favorite books, wines, pictures, and music. Gourmet dining is always available. There is an endless supply of El Diablo cigars. The professor is puzzled. He calls St. Peter. "Has a mistake been made?" "How so?" The

professor describes his sybaritic setting. "That's right, professor." "But how can this be hell?" A pause, and then St. Peter murmurs, "You must share the apartment with a colleague."

10. The full opening passage of lectio 15 of the *Speculum* is: "*Blessed are thou amongst women*. Of the blessedness of our blessed Virgin let us say more, let us hear more. Happy is the blessed Mary, unhappy every damned soul, all those to whom is said, *Depart from me, ye cursed, into eternal fire*. Damned certainly is every vicious soul, and the virtuous Mary is blessed. Damnation comes into the world through the seven capital sins, Mary obtained blessedness through the contrary virtues. O Mary, blessed art thou amongst women. Blessed in humility as opposed to pride, in charity as opposed to envy, in meekness opposed to wrath, in steadiness opposed to sloth, liberality opposed to avarice, sobriety rather than gluttony, and chastity rather than lust" (277b–278a, *Opera* of Bonaventure).

11. This marvelous work has now been ascribed to Conrad of Saxony. See Chiavacci Leonardi in her introduction to her edition of the *Purgatorio*, pp. xxii–xxiii.

12. *Speculum* 278a.

13. There is also a tradition holding that Mary had vowed herself to virginity before the Annunciation. If so, this raises questions about the meaning of her betrothal to Joseph. But by tradition, after the Annunciation, Joseph too having been visited by an angel, both spouses were vowed to virginity.

14. Domenico Bassi, *Il Mese di Maggio con Dante*, p. 19.

15. See Chiavacci Leonardi in her edition of the *Purgatorio*, introduction to canto 10, p. 291.

16. This priority of Christ is never to be forgotten, yet Dante puts Mary forward first when he gives examples of the virtues opposed to the capital sins. We will discuss this later. A sign of our blindness is the temptation to think of Mary as in some way the rival of Her Son. However, if Christ is our primary mediator with the Father, there are secondary mediators as well, and of these Mary is far and away the first. This is not some antic choice of Dante and the Church fathers and doctors on whom he relies, but an ineradicable feature of the providential plan of salvation.

17. See R. P. Cornelii a Lapide, *Commentaria in Quatuor Evangelia*, ed. Antonius Padovani (Turin: Marietti, 1922), Tomus III, p. 201.

18. *ST* IIaIIae, q. 157.

19. Cornelii a Lapide, *Commentaria in Quatuor Evangelia*, Tomus III, p. 125b.

20. In the Latin of the original,

3. Quoniam ipse liberavit me de laqueo venantium, et a verbo aspero.
4. Scapulis suis obumbrabit tibi: et sub pennis ejus sperabis.
5. Scuto circumdabit te veritas ejus: non timebis a timore nocturno,
6. A sagitta volante in die, a negotio perambulante in tenebris: ab incurso, et daemonio meridiano.

21. See Chiavacci Leonardi in her edition of the *Purgatorio*, p. 661, note on line 142.

22. According to Thomas, "Of all the passions the most difficult to regulate by reason is that of pleasure, and especially those natural pleasures constant in our lives such as the pleasures associated with food and drink without which human life is impossible, and many desert the rule of reason in their regard. When desire for such pleasure transcends the rule of reason there is the sin of gluttony, since gluttony is immoderate desire in eating" (*De malo*, q. 15, a. 1, c). One may be reminded of Dr. Johnson's remark that, with respect to alcohol, he found abstinence easier than moderation.

23. See Charles Singleton on this canto, in *The Divine Comedy, Purgatorio*, text and commentary (Princeton: Princeton University Press, 1973), p. 121 of commentary.

24. Thomas puts the burden of this teleology on the father; the father has the primary task of educating the child and preparing it for life, and the mother's nurturing belongs to the early years. Thomas notes that he will not take up here the question of monogamy or the length of a marriage, for a lifetime or not. He does discuss these topics elsewhere and argues that polyandry is clearly wrong: a woman who sleeps with many men will have difficulty knowing which is the father of her child. The case for monogamy is less obvious, and is grounded in the friendship that cohabitation should bring about. That would provide a reason against abandoning a wife once her fruitful years are over and turning to someone younger (or, one may add, abandoning a husband for similar incapacities). But the indissolubility of marriage has its true grounding in Scripture: whom God has joined together, let no man put asunder. On these matters, see *Summa theologiae*, Supplementum, q. 65. Questions 41 through 68, all of them taken from Thomas's earlier commentary on the *Sentences* of Peter Lombard, constitute an extensive treatment of matrimony. Question 15 of *De malo* presupposes this discussion and deals only with the vice of lust.

25. See Teodolinda Barolini, *Dante's Poets, Textuality and Truth in the Comedy* (Princeton: Princeton University Press, 1984).

26. George Santayana, *Three Philosophical Poets: Lucretius, Dante, Goethe*, Harvard Studies in Comparative Literature 1 (Cambridge, Mass.: Harvard University Press, 1927). See also T. S. Eliot, *The Varieties of Metaphysical Poetry*, ed. and introduced by Ronald Schuchard (New York: Harcourt Brace & Co., 1993). See too my Aquinas Lecture, given at Marquette University: *Rhyme and Reason: Saint Thomas and Modes of Discourse* (Milwaukee: Marquette University Press, 1981).

27. See Thomas Aquinas, *Commentary on Aristotle's Posterior Analytics*, trans. and commentary by Richard Berquist (South Bend, Ind.: Dumb Ox Books, 2007).

28. Singleton is doubtless right that this new telos did not entail getting rid of Beatrice, however ambiguous the *Convivio* is when it compares itself to the *Vita Nuova*. In *Convivio* 1.1, comparing his present task with the earlier work, Dante says that now he will treat more *virilmente* what he had treated earlier; the *Vita Nuova* is fervent and passionate, the *Convivio* temperate and

virile. He attributes this to his youth in writing the earlier work, and his maturity now. The contrast has puzzled many, among them myself. In the first chapter I advanced a fancied hypothesis for the fact that the *Convivio*, whose well thought-out plan is given to us early, was left unfinished. Like the *Vita Nuova*, it consists of both poetry and prose, the prose sections being heavy treatises that expound the literal and allegorical meaning of the odes preceding them. The reader is certainly aware that Dante has been to school in the meantime. There is no expression in the *Convivio*, as in the final paragraph of the *Vita Nuova*, of dissatisfaction with what he has done. But dropping the work is perhaps eloquent. He would go on to the *Comedy*, from which prose is absent.

29. Thus, in his work *Orthodoxy*, Chesterton considers original sin a fact, not a dogma.

30. *The Divine Comedy of Dante Alighieri*, Italian and English, trans. with introd. and commentary by Allen Mandelbaum (Berkeley: University of California Press, 1982), vol. 3, *Paradiso*, pp. 60, 62.

31. Ibid., vol. 2, *Purgatorio*, p. 270.

FOUR.   *Queen of Heaven*

1. Chiavacci Leonardi comments: "The simple confession that Dante makes at this point—unique in the poem and in all his work—of his daily prayer is another singular mark of this scene in the *Paradiso*, where the dearest human feelings invade the heaven of inaccessible divine eternity with a profound and almost unavoidable mistake" (the mistake of importing time into eternity). In her edition of the *Paradiso*, p. 641, note to lines 88–90 (my translation).

2. An indulgence for saying the Angelus morning and night was granted by Pope John XXII in 1318, which suggests that the practice was already common. Saying the Angelus at noon came later.

3. During the Pascal season, this antiphon is substituted for the Angelus as the final prayer after Compline.

4. Heb. 11:1. For Dante and St. Thomas, the Vulgate text read: "fides est substantia rerum sperandarum, argumentum non apparentium."

5. Thomas's commentary on Hebrews can be found in *Super Epistolas S. Pauli Lectura*, ed. Raphaelis Cai, O.P., vol. 2 (Turin: Marietti, 1953).

6. Such remarks, frequent enough in Thomas, make efforts to drive a wedge between him and Dante on the matter unconvincing.

7. *Super Epistolas S. Pauli Lectura*, vol. 2, n. 557.

8. Thomas's *De magistro* (On the Teacher), prompted by Augustine's work by the same name, can be found in his *Disputed Questions on Truth* (*De ver.*), q. 11.

9. See *De ver.*, q. 14, a. 1.

10. See *De ver.*, q. 14, a. 9, on the relation of known truths to believed truths. According to Thomas, "it should be said that the way God is demonstrated to be one is not called an article of faith, but is presupposed by the articles, for the knowledge of faith presupposes natural knowledge just as grace

presupposes nature. But the unity of the divine essence, as this is held by the faithful, like providence and universal providence, and the like, which cannot be proved, constitute articles" (q. 14, a. 9, ad 8). More will be said of this later.

11. See Charles De Koninck, *La Piété du Fils: Etudes sur l'Assomption* (Quebec: Les Presses Universitaires Laval, 1954).

12. *I Summa contra gentes*, 3: "Among the things that we *confess* about God there are truths of two kinds" (emphasis added).

13. The assumption is that one cannot know and believe the same truth at the same time and in the same respect. Knowledge follows on proof (or self-evidence), whereas belief reposes on someone's say-so, on authority. The believer who proves the existence of God no longer believes that God exists in the manner that he has proved it. These are, of course, narrow senses of "know" and "believe." Often we speak of what we believe as what we know and of what we know as our beliefs. But these broad senses of the terms do not deny the contrast resulting from their narrower senses.

14. See *I Summa contra gentes*, 4: "If the only path to knowledge of God lay through reason, the human race would be left in the deepest shadows of ignorance." Why? Because only a few can formulate cogent proofs of the preambles, and then with an admixture of error.

15. See Alexander Masseron, "Dante et saint Bernard 'fideles de la Reine du ciel,'" in Masseron, *Dante et saint Bernard* (Paris: Michel, 1953), pp. 71–143.

16. "Constructed, with solemn scansion, of four serious tercets, which already have the note of a conclusion, this prayer summarizes both the external (vv. 80–84) and the inner (v. 85) story that is the object of the entire poem." Chiavacci Leonardi in her edition of the *Paradiso*, p. 864, note to lines 79ff.

17. By his absolute power, as theologians say, God could have chosen any number of alternative ways to save us.

18. We are reminded of a simile from the previous canto: Dante compares Bernard's gaze at Mary to that of a Holy Year pilgrim come to Rome and seeing Veronica's veil with which she wiped the face of Jesus when he was carrying the cross. "Just as one come, from Croatia perhaps, to visit our Veronica, one whose long hunger is now satisfied and who, as long as it is displayed, repeats in thought, 'O my Lord Jesus Christ, true God, was your face then like this image that I now see?'" (*Par.* 31.102–108).

19. All of the following English translations of canto 33 are from Mandelbaum's edition (see chapter 3 notes).

20. One could make the theological point that the only one we can love more than ourselves is God; we love our neighbor as ourselves, that is, called as we are to the beatific vision.

Epilogue

1. The Memorial, in French and Latin, is dated "the year of Grace, 1654, Monday, November 23, feast of St. Clement, pope and martyr, and other

martyrs in the Martyrology; eve of St. Chysogonus, martyr, and others. Between ten-thirty in the evening, more or less, until around half past midnight." *Pascal Oeuvres Complètes*, preface d'Henri Gouhier, présentation et notes de Louis LaFuma (Paris: Éditions du Seuil, 1963), p. 618, my translation.

INDEX

Abelard, Peter, 27
acedia. *See* sloth
Aeneid (Virgil), 26
Agnus Dei, penitents singing, 66
allegorical meaning
    of the *Commedia*, 20, 126
    —in punishment of the proud, 63
    of Scripture, 15
anagogical meaning, 15
    O'Connor, Flannery, on literature
      and, 20–21
    of singing of Psalm 113(114) by
      souls, 35–36
angels. *See also* Gabriel
    hierarchy, 60–61
    —Pseudo-Denis the Areopagite
      and Gregory the Great on, 116
    number of, 117
Angelus prayer, 71, 151n2
anger
    arising out of envy, 45
    as capital sin, 56
    expiation on third level of Purga-
      tory, 41, 42, 66–70
    in Hell, 66
    justified, 68
    meekness as virtue opposite, 58
    Stoics versus Aristotelians on, 68–69
Anna, 131
Annunciation
    humility of Mary and, 59–62
    Luke on, 70
    purity of Mary and, 83
Anselm, Saint, 118
apodictic discourse, 88–89

Aristotelians' quarrel with Stoics on
    anger, 68–69
Aristotle, 27, 28. *See also Nicoma-*
    chean Ethics (Aristotle)
    Book of Problems, 14
    on desire for happiness, 44
    on formal logic of syllogism, 88
    morality and, 123
    on moral philosophy, 22
    Poetics, 21
    —on Platonic dialogues as type of
      poetry, 87
    —on power and range of the
      poetic, 88
    on poetry as imitation, 89
    Posterior Analytics' commentary by
      Thomas Aquinas, 87
    Thomas Aquinas's use of, 117
"Ars poetica" (MacLeish), 20
Augustine, Saint
    Confessions, 41
    on desire for union with God, 123
    on lateness of conversion, 37
    on multiple meanings of
      Scripture, 15
    on original sin, 92, 95
    on Sermon on the Mount, 51
    on virtues of philosophers as vices,
      123
avarice
    beast as, 23
    as capital sin, 55
    examples of, 76
    expiation on fifth level of Purga-
      tory, 76–79

155

RALPH McINERNY
is professor of philosophy and the Michael P. Grace Professor
of Medieval Studies at the University of Notre Dame.

He is author and editor of numerous books, including
his autobiography, *I Alone Have Escaped to Tell You*
(University of Notre Dame Press, 2006), and the first two
volumes of *The Writings of Charles De Koninck*
(University of Notre Dame Press, 2008, 2009).